U Empath You

Universal Messages and Personal Stories
Bringing Inspiration and Resources for You

Compiled By
Rebecca Saltman
Jade Rehder

Powerful You!
PUBLISHING
Sharing Wisdom ~ Shining Light

U Empath You

Universal Messages and Personal Stories Bringing Inspiration and Resources for You

Copyright © 2022

The authors of this book do not dispense medical advice or prescribe the use of any technique as a form of treatment for physical, emotional, or medical problems without the advice of a physician, either directly or indirectly. Nor is this book intended to provide personalized legal, accounting, financial, or investment advice. Readers are encouraged to seek the counsel of competent professionals with regards to such matters. The intent of the authors is to provide general information to individuals who are taking positive steps in their lives for emotional and spiritual well-being. If you use any of the information in this book for yourself, which is your constitutional right, the authors and the publisher assume no responsibility for your actions.

Published by: Powerful You! Inc. USA
powerfulyoupublishing.com

Library of Congress Control Number: 2022903815

Rebecca Saltman and Jade Rehder – First Edition

ISBN: 978-1-7356579-9-8

First Edition April 2022

Self-Help

Table of Contents

Table of Contents

Dear Isabelle,

Knowing you on this journey is a precious gift. Thank you for saying yes and gently coaxing our genius into the open where it may shine.

Love,
Andy

10-30-2022

Foreword

The first time I heard the word "empath" I was watching *Star Trek: The Next Generation* with my family as a young boy in the late 1980s. It was one of our most beloved TV shows. The starship's counselor, Deanna Troi, was half-human and half-Betazoid, an alien species that possessed powerful psychic abilities. Since she was only half-blooded, her psychic powers were reduced to the ability to sense emotions and other energy patterns, and for other psychic beings to speak with her across space.

Fast forward to me at age forty, being coached by my friend and colleague, Stephanie Red Feather, in a program called *Embrace Your Empath* that provides guidance and practical tools for empaths to protect our energy and hone our skills. Stephanie helped me understand that I was not alone in my ability to sense emotions and energy from people, animals, and other life forms. She also explained that it was common to feel confused, and often hurt, when empaths are unaware of how this energy interacts with the world around us, which can lead—as it did in my case—to various defense patterns like numbing and avoidance. Prior to training with Stephanie, I credit my early empath awareness to David Sauvage.

> *"For most empaths, suppression becomes our modus operandi. In order to cope in our families, societies, and the world at large, we take our precious uniqueness and banish it...we made an unconscious decision that it is safer to tuck it away and pretend we are someone else."*
> ~*The Evolutionary Empath, Rev. Stephanie Red Feather, Ph.D.*

Empaths are not limited to science fiction, though it's notable that television writers understood so little about us in the late twentieth century that we were portrayed as an alien race, and typically female. I'm also a lifelong fan of Star Wars, being deeply drawn to the mindful energy of the Jedi and regularly donning an Obi-Wan Kenobi robe and lightsaber when each new movie is released. While they were not described as "empaths," the Jedi spend their entire lives cultivating skills related to sensing and channeling the power of the energy all around us. While female Jedi were graciously introduced later, the characters I grew up with were all male, and brought a warrior edge to the idea of energy sensitivity.

Thankfully, academic science is catching up due to the groundbreaking research of Dr. Elaine Aron and her husband, Dr. Arthur Aron, who published their first book, *The Highly Sensitive Person* (HSP), in 1996. They recognized four distinct traits of high sensitivity, or "DOES" (Depth of processing, Overstimulation, Empathy/Emotional responsiveness and being Sensitive to the Subtle). Interestingly, they are revising their framework after realizing that it focused mostly on the overstimulation aspect, which is really the only negative one. I understand why this bias would overshadow all the incredible gifts of being an empath, because the world is just beginning to gain clarity about those gifts, and empaths are slowly learning how to manage our energy so that we can be stable enough to reveal them.

I learned in an HSP training for coaches that the Arons researched more than one hundred species of animals and discovered that about twenty percent of each population was highly sensitive. Horses are particularly so, and even know how to deploy their most sensitive comrades as sentries on the outskirts of the herd in order to detect and relay threats. My great hope is that humans also learn the best ways to support empaths for our gifts to shine, so that we may be fully expressed and that all of humanity may benefit from our unique powers.

American socialization (and others) sadly marginalizes empaths from every walk of life, as our culture generally conditions us to embrace more masculine ways of being in order to survive and succeed. This seems especially destructive for boys and male-identifying people, who are often demanded to hide and deny being empaths, while girls and women tend to be more accepted in their sensitivity. While this cultural phenomenon may have allowed the extraordinary contributors of this book more access to explore being empaths than their male counterparts, it also has grave limitations in a world that views emotional sensitivity and caregiving as a weakness, and for millennia has treated females as inferior to males. Thankfully, my sensitivity as a boy was typically encouraged by both my parents, which is likely the main reason I'm here writing this today.

It's worth mentioning that I am a large-bodied, cis-gendered, straight white American man writing the foreword to a book of essays written entirely by people who identify as women. Using the HSP research as a reference, there is no biological connection between being an empath and any other identity or culture. A limited perspective of human liberation focused on wealth and security heralds white men as the beneficiaries of systems that serve us well. A richer view reveals how the systems to which we cling are hurting us as well – they stifle our emotional range of expression, limit deep connection, reduce human intimacy and lead to an endless array of distracting material and superficial means to fill the empty holes we carry around.

This can raise a bit of a conflict as I engage with people in diverse activist spaces who often see my visible privileges and don't see this invisible quality of being an empath. There is rarely the time and space needed to unpack how this affects me, and I don't have a label or diagnosis to share, even though I'm sure those are never sufficient to convey a person's way of meeting the world. As we are learning to build a lexicon to describe many identities in an attempt to build a more equitable world, the notions of being an empath or energetically sensitive rarely seem to make the list. It's especially confusing given the importance of identifying and de-centering people who have systemic privileges, but have not yet entered the deep emotional journey to dismantle and heal their own reactiveness to challenging interactions around racism, sexism, ableism, ageism, etc. It's easy to mistake the sensitivity of being an empath for the fragility of dominant culture, which doesn't leave much room for true expression or healing.

The number of marginalized identities one holds typically increases the amount of energy spent to interact with the world, so I recognize that being an empath is but one window into how hard it is to explain an invisible "condition." Most people are unfamiliar with the term "empath," or what it means to live this way. The empath remains a mystery even to those who embody it, devoid of terminology that could render any meaningful level of understanding. The Highly Sensitive Person has recently been designated as a form of neurodiversity, so that feels like some progress toward inclusion and recognition, and perhaps a clearer path for me to build trusting relationships with people who choose to understand, respect, and accommodate this quality. The truth is, I live in fear most of the time. I'm often breathless moving about the world, and terrified when entering a room full of people whose energies will likely bombard me. Yet I fight for an inclusive society not only for my own sake, but because I realize I have it easier than so many people who hold multiple identities that are marginalized. My privileges afford me a considerable amount of energetic insulation.

"Boundaries are the distance at which I can love you and me simultaneously." ~ Prentis Hemphill

The only sustainable way to overcome what often feels like an assault on my energy is to manage my boundaries and practice self-care. In many ways, this is still a work in progress for me and I imagine it always will be. It requires consistent attention. One label that is often intermingled with the concept of empath is that of introvert. They are not the same terrain, since introvert and extrovert relate to how we reclaim our energy, the former by being alone and the latter from other people. I consider myself an introvert because I need alone time to recharge my energy. I am a very social person, though not wildly outspoken. Sometimes my desire to be social outweighs my need for energy and self-care, leaving me depleted and my energetic boundaries porous and susceptible to even more fracturing if not mended.

When I don't manage my boundaries well, I sometimes have less empathy. I can feel attacked and more reactive. This may seem like a contradiction, but being an empath and having empathy are not the same thing. Empathy is a learned trait, and something everyone should invest time in developing. It is the art of relating to another person's feelings through one's own lived experience. No two people will ever completely understand the other's experience. That's part of being human. However if we make the time to try, most of us can find a path to relate emotionally. By contrast, being an empath is an evolutionary trait that carries innate gifts and challenges. The ability to sense another person's emotions can certainly help with empathy, when we maintain proper boundaries and energy hygiene.

Before I had any language to understand or explain living as an empath, or had taken the numerous years to dive deep into my consciousness to understand how I came to be, I turned down the road that is common for those who feel assaulted by the world's energies, whether as an empath or other marginalized identity. I used marijuana, sex, and food as means of numbing in order to reduce anxiety from unknown sources. I now know that there are ways to manage my energy through good sleep, meditation, breathing, and body work, for example. And let's be real, disassociation in moderation can be a form of self-care as well.

There are two areas that continue to perplex me as an empath. The first is what I consider to be the final frontier of consciousness work—romance! One of the unfortunate byproducts of my early avoidance strategy was retreating from areas that felt painful in a relationship, often resulting in shutting down or withdrawing. This is how I spent many of my early relationships, not understanding why I so often felt hurt or misunderstood by the women I dated. Now that I've done considerable work in this area to meet a mate's energy, and embrace tension of all kinds, I've noticed a new problem. The women I meet don't seem to have much experience or knowledge about how to interact with a highly sensitive man, and might even be conditioned to find it less attractive in a hyper-masculine world. I wonder whether two empaths are better off together or if a balance of different kinds of energy sensitivity would typically lead to a healthier relationship.

The second area that can feel confusing is knowing the difference between sensing and stories, which are typically based on fear or projections that I've constructed from past experiences. Managing my energy, boundaries, and presence are the best tools I've found to help me ensure that I am truly sensing a person's energy rather than making up a story about them, but it's hard to be completely certain all the time. Studying mindfulness, conscious leadership, Spaceholding, True Purpose®, Heart of Business, Shakti Leadership, and other methods of integrating these energies has helped me to cultivate a deeper awareness. When I know which energy I'm sensing, I'm better equipped to navigate any situation.

Much of my work in the world is building communities of care where people enjoy dignity and agency together. The foundation of these communities is authentic relationships. We need new kinds of skills to co-create a just and sustainable future, particularly the ability to hold space for healing, emergence, and justice. Empaths are naturally suited to this work as we are able to read the energy of a room and detect subtleties that most people cannot. Deep healing work is done in the trauma body, and also benefits from people who are able to detect, transform, and release somatic energy patterns.

I hope this book is the first of its kind – shining a bright light on pioneering empaths who tell their own stories of moving through the world. I hope more men discover and embrace their empath nature and are moved to tell their stories. I hope that we continue to develop understanding for the empath and all marginalized and invisibilized identities, especially at younger ages, so that we learn to move at the speed of care.

My dream is for humans to understand the extraordinary power of empaths, and our importance for nurturing a healthy, equitable, joyful, and loving humanity. Only in times of relative peace could such a subtle trait be encouraged to thrive and be recognized for its importance. May we all be so lucky to live in that time.

~ Andy Swindler

ABOUT ANDY: Andy brings hearts together to unify humanity. He envisions a world that embraces healthy tensions to ensure dignity and agency for every person. Andy is devoted to building an equitable world by navigating his own complicity in systems of oppression while transforming them. He coaches via Lead From Love and co-founded FeelReal.net to hold space for people to share our true stories and connect deeply in authentic community to shift the dominant narrative from fear to love. Andy is immersed in mutual aid and restorative justice communities in Chicago and enjoys percussion, piano, photography, cycling, rock climbing, and embroidery craftivism.

andyswindler.com

Fire Up Clap

This practice is based on the train clap, which is a favorite motivational tool among facilitators at trainings and seminars. For example, they may use the Fire Up Clap to get a crowd (sometimes hundreds or even thousands of people) to raise their energy and get moving after lunch. You know how you feel after having eaten quickly then rush back to your seat knowing you'll be sitting for hours. You can feel sluggish, unfocused, and unmotivated to pay attention. I know there have been times when I could have used more energy to take action, complete a task, or move faster in my day. How about you?

We have all been through a time of less movement and now is the time to increase the inner flame.

The Fire Up Clap has always reminded us of a pep rally. You are cheering yourself on. Let's get fired up, up, up, up!

Fire Up Clap

- Stand up.
- Start clapping your hands slowly.
- Increase the speed of the clapping with each clap until you are clapping as fast as you can.
- Feel the amount of energy you are creating inside your body.
- Visualize storing the fire energy you have created in your internal oven between your second and third energy center.

- Feel what it is like to increase your internal fire and personal drive.

- Throw your right arm in the air then pull your arm down and yell, "Fire Up!"

- Repeat the practice until you have your energy Fired Up to the level you want and it feels good!

You will find that this practice assists you in increasing your enthusiasm, expanding your courage, and increasing your productivity. You will digest food more easily. Your vision will be clearer and you will move faster.

Special Inspiration

Confused about what your purpose is in life? Repeat this practice each morning for thirty days and allow your internal fire to inspire you to live your purpose. It will help you notice what comes into your experience each day, whether new or repeatedly, be it a thought, a sound, a person, a place, a thing, a feeling, or an idea. Lean in to what the fire energy is bringing you to fuel the power of your dreams.

Introduction

em·path
/ˈempaTH/
noun
(chiefly in science fiction) a person with the paranormal ability to apprehend the mental or emotional state of another individual.

It is fascinating that the first definition that comes up when you search the word "empath" mentions that it is "chiefly in science fiction." It reads almost like a disclaimer, a red flag to the researcher saying, "Just so you know, this stuff belongs in fantasy land!" Perhaps that explains why we empaths prefer to spend our time reading and watching science fiction rather than anything in "the real world." After all, if the Oxford Dictionary doesn't consider our experiences to be "real," who is going to believe anything different?

As we searched further, we found this…

"What exactly does it mean to be an empath?

*An empath is **someone who feels more empathy than the average person**. These people are usually more accurate in recognizing emotions by looking at another person's face. They are also more likely to recognize emotions earlier than other people and rate those emotions as being more intense."*

This certainly is better than Oxford, and yet it is still far off when it comes to describing how we might experience the world.

We have been spending quite a bit of time thinking about and speaking to others about what it means to be an empath in these times. We have been discussing the gifts and pitfalls that empaths experience in various situations and with regard to topics such as grief, blame, shame, attachments, celebrations, joy, and so much more. Not surprisingly, we learned that the journeys, while unique, also shared some commonalities, one of which is the sense of isolation and having to "follow the breadcrumbs."

Yes, trust is essential to any spiritual journey; that said, part of the isolation comes from the fact that many, if not most, empaths come into awareness that they are a "sensitive" only to find that they don't have resources or support around their newfound understanding. It was this need for community, a safe space where their stories are normalized, that spoke to us and made us realize that sharing experiences, resources, and tips among other empaths and sensitives (in live, online, and video settings) would be a great gift, both to those new to the fold and those who have been consciously walking this path their whole lives.

We realized that it is now time to do what we can to bring together the stories, experiences, and, more importantly, learnings from empaths near and far so that folks wouldn't feel so isolated, alone, or only "part of science fiction."

Please understand that these stories and resources are just the tip of the iceberg when it comes to empathic experiences. It is our hope that this book will open the door for many others to step into their "superpowers" and to share the beauty and the challenges that come with those gifts with the world. Maybe, just maybe, it will create such a ripple effect that one day Oxford will change their definition of what it means to be an empath, or at least remove their disclaimer!

~ Jade and Rebecca

Empath Types and Qualities

The following definitions are derived from our collective experiences and have been included for the purpose of providing context to the chapters ahead. That said, we know that many definitions for empathic gifts exist and we truly honor all views. We invite you to read with an open mind and take what resonates and assists you on your journey.

Emotional

Emotional Empaths naturally pick up and embody others' emotions, and often unknowingly take them on as their own.

How does this show up?

If you're an Emotional Empath, you often know what others are feeling although these feelings are unexpressed or discussed out loud. Large crowds and/or emotionally-charged events (like family fights or rival sporting events) can be oppressive and/or overwhelming for you. You also pick up on people who unknowingly project their emotions onto others, even from vast distances, which is quite uncomfortable. Like many Emotional Empaths, you might have difficulties with "gut stuff" that leads you to take over-the-counter remedies, generally without success. You may also be told that you are "too" emotional by others.

Physical

Physical empaths feel in their own bodies what is going on physically for others, including pain.

How does this show up?

The experiences of Physical Empaths are as varied as people

walking the Earth. These can be mild, such as picking up on the stiff knee of a stranger who walks past you in a mall, or intense, like someone's heart palpitations. Because of this, you may find it especially difficult to be in hospitals, nursing homes, or on land where violent events have occurred.

Earth

Earth Empaths feel the physical symptoms emanating from the planet. This may include things like earthquakes, erupting volcanoes, hurricanes, tornadoes, or even something as simple as a very windy day or a heavy rainstorm.

How does this show up?

As an Earth Empath, you may feel something like anxiety, shaking, or feeling out of balance in advance of an earthquake. You may also get headaches that are unusual in type or severity, back pain, digestive issues, and other physical ailments. After the earth event happens you often feel relief from those symptoms and experiences.

Collective/Universal

The Collective Empath feels what is happening with the planet and its inhabitants as a whole; for example, the stress and anxiety of people and animals involved in an "event" (flood/social unrest/wildfire) even if it is thousands of miles away. They also often pick up what is happening in the astrological world and sun activity before it is revealed.

How does this show up?

As a Collective Empath, you focus on emotions from a global perspective, and, similar to the Earth Empath, experience relief from uncomfortable emotions once the crisis or event subsides and those affected are being taken care of. Things like solar flares may also affect you mentally, emotionally, and physically, and planetary shifts such as retrogrades and oppositions can be very disruptive.

Knower/Intuitive/Claircognizant

Knower Empaths have a greater field of awareness, which allows them to access information (in advance or real-time) related to a given situation. They are often called "human lie detectors" because they know instinctively when others are being dishonest or not revealing something, which is experienced as a "yes" or "no" (also referred to as "trusting their gut").

How does this show up?

If you're a Knower/Intuitive/Claircognizant Empath, you feel or simply know things, often without knowing how. In addition, you are able to pull ideas and solutions to challenges seemingly from the ethers, even when you have no experience or previous knowledge of the subject. Others may call you a "mind reader" because you often answer questions before they are asked out loud. To put it bluntly, you KNOW things and SCARE those who don't!

As a Knower, you may often be inclined to share what you know with others and can struggle with the need to be right. You feel amazing when you wait for then your wisdom is more readily received.

Medium/Psychic

Medium or Psychic Empaths have the ability to communicate with different spirits. Though these spirits are usually those of deceased individuals, some Medium Empaths can also see or sense energies from other realms of consciousness and alternative realities.

How does this show up?

More than twenty years after *The Sixth Sense* was released, the line "I see dead people" remains one of the most popular in film history. While your experiences may not be as dramatic as those of the young boy in the film, you can often hear, sense, or even see spirits of those who have passed away. You also may be able to see through the veil between the seen and unseen world—including the realms of fairies, elves, leprechauns—and see and sense unusual wildlife and plant forms living in these alternate realities.

Dream/Precognitive

Precognitive empaths are highly intuitive beings with the ability to see, feel, and know into the future, often experiencing a situation or event before it even happens.

How does this show up?

If you're a Dream/Precognitive Empath, you are very sensitive to the energies around you. This shows up in various ways, from déjà vu moments to precognitive dreams. You may also, during emotional, visual, and physical disturbances, "pick up" clues of changes and danger that less sensitive people are unable to read or understand.

Heyoka

The word Heyoka means "sacred clown" or "spiritual fool" in the Lakota and Dakota Native American dialects. Heyoka empaths are said to be the rarest and most powerful variety, acting as a spiritual mirror to those around them to assist in their growth. These often misunderstood empaths are catalysts for transformation, providing a more direct route to change that works for all.

How does this show up?

As a Heyoka empath, you are able to tune into popular points of view of those surrounding you, mirror these ideas back, and then point out the flaws. As a result, you are often labeled as "disruptive." You don't do this to be difficult, rather, it is coming from your deep sensitivities and knowledge. You look at, and experience, the world differently, and challenge others to do the same.

The world whispers to you, "you cannot withstand the storm." You whisper back "I am the storm."

Animal

Animal Empaths intuit the emotions and physical feelings of all kinds of animals, near and far.

How does this show up?

If you're an Animal Empath, you may find it difficult to be around animals under stress or anxiety, for example, when they are caged in a shelter. Even watching stories about animals being lost, abandoned, or harmed is deeply upsetting and may be completely avoided. You may have the capacity to sense animals' thoughts and feelings and convey this information to their owners, thus facilitating a more harmonious time together.

Plant

Plant Empaths receive communication from plants and foliage of many kinds.

How does this show up?

House plants may call to you for water. Trees in the forest may communicate their wisdom and share their energy with you. You often feel the loss of trees and forests cut down by the logging industry; however, you may also have the capacity to create "calm" in natural habitats that have been negatively impacted by sharing your loving consciousness with the area.

Clear Touch/Psychometric

Psychometric Empaths have the ability to receive detailed information and energy from inanimate objects like photographs and jewelry. These empaths can also sense the origins of something, its meaning, and its age.

How does this show up?

This can come about when you touch an item, sit in a chair, or step onto land that still has "energy" around it. The messages may be received in many different ways, through your extrasensory gifts.

Empathic Energy Communication

Innately, Empaths have some of each of the above "types" (emotional, physical, animal, et cetera) in their makeup, and most who see themselves in those definitions have already awakened to their gifts. While being an empath is often viewed as a psychic ability, we ask you to consider it through a wider lens—as an invitation to be on an EMpoweredPATH in this life. It is the journey of bringing your expanded consciousness and gifts of awareness into your body and daily experience while remaining in the awareness that you are one aspect of the whole weave of humanity. As such, Empaths are also in connection with their extrasensory perception network, or—as we like to call it—"Spiritual ESPN" channels, as both "Receivers" and Transmitters."

Receiver Empaths pick up the emotions, energies, and messages of "projective people," those who are sending energy and emotion out from their personal energy field. Imagine that a Receiver can see the energy ripple out from the center of the projector. Receivers are often labeled highly sensitive, overly sensitive, "cry babies," and "drama queens." Most Empaths are over fifty percent receiver.

Transmitting Empaths naturally and actively transmit their emotions outward, most often when triggered, so that others will feel them. Immature Transmitting Empaths sometimes use this gift to manipulate and get what they want.

Navigating the
Empath Tools in this Book
Self Guided Solutions for Your Path of Wellbeing

It is our belief and desire that energy hygiene should be taught in every school; in the meantime, we at U Empath You are on it! This book includes more than twenty D-I-Y energy practices to support you in enjoying your life as an empowered empath. As empaths, we have the capacity to tap out of the loops and swoops that create overloads for our emotions, thoughts, incoming energy/ messages, and the waves of the collective humanity. We also know that with conscious awareness of our energy patterning, we have the opportunity to move into the capacity of our multidimensional selves.

Instead of telling you what to do and when to do it, these visualizations and exercises will assist you in working with your physical, emotional, mental, and spiritual energy. We think of them like recipes, or combinations of ingredients and information gained in multiple places. So try them, find a few that work well for you, and use them to create a daily energy routine or ritual. Most importantly, spice them up with your own knowledge and wisdom to make them your own.

Much of the foundation for these practices come out of Jade's training as an NLP trainer and an alaka'i of Ancient Hawaiian Huna la'au kahea. To Kumu Maggie Connor of Hawaii Ko Aloha, with whom Jade trained, we offer a heartfelt "Mahalo nui loa, Maggie for being an outstanding way-shower!"

Our goal is to provide you with useful self-guided solutions to working with your empathic gifts and overall energy in ways that may be useful in attaining energetic wellness. This is not to be seen or perceived as medical advice in any way. It is complementary to any other forms of emotional or mental support you are receiving. No medical advice is given.

CHAPTER 1

Is Life a Fairytale
or Is the Fairytale Life?
Rebecca Saltman

"Fairy tales are more than true: not because they tell us that dragons exist, but because they tell us that dragons can be beaten." ~ Neil Gaiman

Sometimes, when sharing our deepest, most secret experiences, it helps to fictionalize them, perhaps even make them into fairytales. And then there are those mystical experiences that seem as unexplainable as a magic trick or journey into mystical realms; however, that doesn't make them any less real...

Once upon a time, in a place far, far away, was a planet called Earth. The third planet from a dazzling sun, Earth was so very beautiful, with sparkling blue skies, luscious green forests, and waters so clean and clear you saw your reflection as you walked by. These waters would cool you in the heat and warm you in the cold. This faraway place also had a mysterious underside, with waters that would rise so high they could swallow the land whole, stunning mountains that sometimes had smoke and fire coming out of them, and land that looked much like many other places, only to shake and split under your feet without warning.

This amazing blue marble in the sky was ruled by its Mother, who was known across lands and cultures by many different names like Ala, Atria, Demeter, Durga, Earth Mother, and Pachamama. For this story, we will call her Gaia.

Gaia was the most magical being in the Universe, and She spent her infinite time and attention, caring deeply for Herself and Her magnificent planet. Her care covered MANY enchanted things, but Her favorite activity was bringing gifted and talented beings of all sorts, sizes, shapes, and colors to Earth. You see, Gaia believed this place was a rare gift and wanted a diverse assortment of exquisite beings to inhabit her. She knew and appreciated that all things were interconnected, like an intricate spider web. She also knew that some beings naturally understood this and, sadly, some did not.

One day, Gaia decided to decorate the earth with Her most favorite beings—SENSITIVE HUMANS!

After going through all the outstanding possibilities, She chose one hundred very unique sensitives, whose talents and abilities were far-reaching. These beings, she mused, would be the perfect earthkeepers who also understood the "spider web." They would be able to connect to other humans, plants, animals, inanimate objects, and even Gaia Herself!

What a gift to all worlds, she thought.

Gaia dreamt that these wondrous new beings could even help Her, for She too was a living creature and often had the same kinds of problems people have. Sometimes, she got sick with fever, sneezed, coughed, belched, had chills, and even shook…

Then She saw her, one of the sensitives, a sweet and innocent baby girl who reminded Gaia of Herself when She was a new creation, something she had long forgotten…

"Empaths did not come into this world to be victims, we came to be warriors. Be brave. Stay strong. We need all hands on deck." ~ Anthon St. Maarten

Once there was a happy, very shy girl with ringlet curls and freckles. The first child born to loving parents, she was a summer baby who loved the water so much it was said she swam before she walked.

The small family grew and the girl had a sister, who she adored. When the Elder was three she became very ill, with tiny evil germs that invaded her blood and raised her body's thermostat to one hundred and four degrees!

Frantic, her parents rushed Elder to the doctor, who immediately sent her to the hospital—she was *that* ill. Miraculously, the little girl survived, and the family was so very grateful to the doctors and nurses who had worked tirelessly to save her.

With each day she continued to grow stronger, yet her mother regularly "hovered," fearing her precious daughter may become sick once again. Instead, the girl grew more and more sensitive. She would become upset while watching a cartoon where someone was sad, she worried about everything around her, and she would become anxious with no provocation; she even cried if someone near to her got hurt. To avoid this pain, the girl started to withdraw, and the Mother now worried that she had become a "wallflower." In truth, the girl wasn't a wallflower at all, she was intuitive and a deep feeler, who quietly listened to and absorbed everything around her.

"Highly sensitive people learned early in life to try to control the external world as a way to attempt to manage their inner one." ~ Sheryl Paul

Outsiders didn't notice anything different about the girl; they merely observed that she was very good, kind, and so well behaved. And though her parents continued to wonder why the Elder was so quiet, she did so well in school and played so nicely with others that eventually they decided she was just "sensitive" and resumed life as it was.

As the children matured the Younger needed an outlet for her creativity and the parents gave her the magical world of theatre. This proved to be such an amazing experience for the Younger that the parents invited the Elder to join this magical world as well. It was a place where both girls thrived, where everything was possible and being "sensitive" was not a problem, but a gift.

The Elder attracted an assortment of fascinating people to her, people of all sizes, shapes, and colors who outside the magical world were considered weirdos, oddballs, and misfits. As the Elder's sensitivities grew, she also grew to love her magical friends and had a very difficult time understanding why they were often ignored or bullied.

The Elder became fiercely protective of these kindred souls. She regularly recognized their gifts and talents and reflected those sensational abilities back to them, which made them all more confident and vibrant. With her merry gang the Elder flourished and was able to do IMPRESSIVE, unheard-of things in this world where everything was possible.

As time passed, Elder was presented with new, incredible opportunities to use her sensitivities. She would see challenges before they happened, she could read people's feelings and thoughts, and she even grew anxious when something bad was going to happen.

The magical world praised and loved the Elder for her exceptional gifts. The outside world, well, that was an entirely different story.

"Now, more than ever, our society is in need of sensitive and empathic people. Now, more than ever, the human race needs to go inwards and connect with the Soul again. As natural-born healers, intuitives, and mentors, it is not only our responsibility but also our destiny to help humanity heal."
~ Aletheia Luna

As the Elder grew into adulthood, she chose to accept the responsibility that all creatures in her realm are given. She would move through the outside world and expose those in it to the idea that Gaia represents: We are all one. The people in the outside world often told her that she needed to "grow up," that the magical world is for children, that she should do "real" things and stop pretending. And though she resisted this advice for some time, the Elder, without even realizing it, got worn down and fell into the ways of the outside world. She found this world colorless, magicless, and it made her deeply depressed.

Even as she grew more and more unhappy, her sensitivities were becoming more and more acute. Without the aid of the magical world it all become too much, and she was called "overly sensitive," dramatic, and even a freak.

Deep inside, she knew that all of these people had no idea what they were talking about, and she began to wonder, *If I was happy as a child and loved all things water, have I literally become a "fish out of water"?*

Then the Elder began waking up in the middle of the night in utter panic. By this time she had all but forgotten the magical world, and she began to listen to the outside world, which was telling her she was too stressed, that she should consider slowing down, taking a few days off; maybe, they said, she should seek help. They decided they must "diagnose" her.

She sought out other people's opinions and points of view and, putting all her magic aside, went to see a doctor. Immediately recognizing that the Elder was struggling, the doctor carefully listened as she described waking up in the middle of the night with anxiety, feeling others' pain, and becoming upset by things happening in the world around her. The doctor was lovely and she did what she knew how to do: she gave the Elder a medicine that would make her feel better.

The Elder was compliant; she didn't ask questions and she took the medicine the doctor gave her. The medicine didn't take the anxiety and pain away—it just made her dreamy, like she was floating in clouds, and not like herself at all. Finally, after months and months, she stopped taking the medicine and went back to feeling like herself, but the anxiety remained.

Shortly after she stopped taking the medication, the Elder's physical health started to deteriorate. She began to suffer terrible belly pain, cramps, and bleeding. Again, she went to a doctor, who also did her best and gave her a pill to take. The Elder yielded and took the pill every day, but all it did was rob her joy and make her grumpy. Clearly, this wasn't the answer either, so she went back to the doctor and asked if there was something else.

This time the doctor said, "You need an operation and that will fix what ails you." Elder gave in, had the first operation, and, for a time, she felt better. Then the physical pain—and the distress—came back, and the Elder chose to have another surgery, with the same result. This cycle repeated again and again; each time the doctors said surgery was the answer, each time the pain came back worse than before. Finally, the Elder decided she couldn't live like this anymore. Her eighth surgery wasn't like the others; it would take away all the things that created her pain, but also the things that gave her what she believed was hope. To the outer world, this operation was a success—the Elder was finally out of physical pain and she no longer bled—but although the Elder was grateful for this, she also felt empty.

Ubuntu: an African word meaning "I am because we are." If one of us is not okay, none of us is...

Then, in those darkest moments, something incredible happened. The Elder started meeting amazing new people who saw her sensitivities as gifts. They explained to her that they too had sensitivities, and they asked her about hers. Together they discovered that the Elder felt anxiety when Gaia had a fever and shook, or when the mountains emitted smoke and fire. These graceful souls reminded her of the magical world where she grew up, where she had flourished.

She explored so many things with her new friends! One day they all took off their shoes and socks and played in the mud. They could hear Gaia talking to them, teaching them how special they were. As if by magic, they all started to wake up from the outside world's dream, the dream that we are all separate from each other. They began to remember that all things are connected on this beautiful earth and that was why their gifts were so very critical.

The most important thing the Elder learned, with the help of her wise new posse, was that when she recognized and aligned herself with her magic and with Gaia, she could feel well and whole again.

And Gaia smiled in joy and relief, knowing that the sweet and innocent baby girl and her magical compadres were on Earth to help her with their amazing gifts.

ABOUT THE AUTHOR: Rebecca Saltman is a writer, earth empath, visionary of change, and rabble-rouser for good whose purpose is to help establish a world that is equitably distributed and where all women are seen, heard, and believed. Twenty-two years ago, Rebecca founded a social entrepreneurial and media justice organization that bridges the needs of business, government, nonprofits, academia, and media to redefine systems that no longer serve the collective. She describes her work as *seeing* past today to the opportunities of tomorrow; *trusting* in a better future so hard that it becomes possible; *weaving* vision, connection, and *healing* the system on every level.

Rebecca Saltman
Disrupt for Good
disruptforgood.life
rebecca@disruptforgood.life
linkedin.com/in/rebeccasaltman

A, B, Cs

Have you ever woken up in the middle of the night after having a terrible dream, or out of nowhere, in a total panic?

If you are an Earth Empath, for example, you may have experienced events like earthquakes, volcanoes, tornadoes, or even political unrest that rattles your body and gives you anxiety. This often happens at very inconvenient times, including, as mentioned above, when you are trying to rest and recharge. Oftentimes you can't get back to sleep because you don't know what the panic is about.

Well, help has arrived, thanks to our dear friend and healer, Doug Jones, who taught us about the A, B, Cs of navigating these situations!

The "A" stands for your "advance team." (Think of the entourage surrounding presidents, royalty, and other VIPs.) Their job is to go to a space/place beforehand and use all the technology and tricks at their disposal to make sure it's SAFE for you to enter.

The "B" can stand for bodyguard, bouncer, or—if you prefer—bartender! Imagine going into a bar late at night—we've all done that, right? Usually the bartender and the bouncer in these places are highly connected and very aware of what's going on in the crowd. If a fight is about to break out, the bartender signals the bouncer, who runs in, takes care of business, and throws the offenders out while your bodyguard gets you to safety. Now, imagine having a bouncer at your bedroom door and a bodyguard to protect you.

The "C" stands for your personal concierge. If you've ever been in a high-end hotel or VIP airport lounge, you know what we're talking about. You just tell this person what you need and they take care of EVERYTHING for you, including hiring the bodyguard, bouncer, and advance team. For example, before going to bed you might say, "Concierge, please make sure my sleep space is safe and undisturbed. Just take a message and let me know in the morning." Yes, you want to know about earthquakes or volcanoes and be of service, but you also know you need your rest and that there is nothing you can do about it in the middle of the night.

You can put these requests on auto repeat; for example, every time you walk into an important meeting or grocery store, just say, "A, B, C" and your team will be on it! You can also create new requests any time you need them.

CHAPTER 2

Doctor Heal Thyself

Being an Empath in Service to People and Planet
Sharon Montes, M.D.

W hat does it mean to live as a soul expressing yourself through a mammalian body? What does it mean to live as an empath, a soul in a body that's especially sensitive to the energies of people, plants, animals, and the planet? How can we take this sensitivity, which can easily lead us to experience life as a series of uncomfortable emotional and physical symptoms, to celebrate our body wisdom and experience more JOY and FREEDOM in our bodies and lives?

Although I work as a holistic doctor, I am the child of a scientist father and an artist mother. My personal understanding, awareness, and personal practices around being an empath draw from science, spirituality, and experiences with psychics and energy healers. In this writing, I will share some of the lessons that have helped me and others move through empathic sensory overwhelm and live on purpose with greater health and happiness.

My first conscious encounter with what it means to be an "empath" happened over thirty years ago. After completing my Family Medicine residency at a regional trauma center, I was burned out; I had also lost touch with my intuition, which had been part of my sensory system since childhood. In my journey of recovery, I was introduced to the book *You Are Psychic!: The Free Soul Method.* The author, Pete A. Sanders Jr., proposes that there are four soul or psychic senses–clairvoyance (seeing), clairaudience (hearing), clairsentience (sensations/empathy), and intuition—all of which are extensions of the physical sensory-receiving organs we already have. Depending on our life purpose, we are stronger in one or two of these soul senses. We all can expand the range of what we perceive. Though soul senses are as natural as breathing, most of us do not recognize how we use our expanded awareness and lack the tools to learn how to consciously develop, manage and use these senses.

I had "burned out" my expanded capacity for empathy and intuition through thousands of hours of left-brain training, trauma work, and inappropriately taking responsibility for others. Sanders' book was foundational in supporting my conscious recovery and the rebuilding of my soul senses. It also helped me accept and understand that clairvoyance wasn't my strongest sense. Hmm... visualize? It was much more accurate and faster for me to bottom-line know and confirm with body sensation. (Although I do find it fun to work with clairvoyants, as my nervous system can plug into their capacity to experience visions and colors.)

This new perspective was also useful in helping me better understand my family's collection of soul senses. Artist mom has clairvoyance and processes information through light and color. Scientist dad is a clairaudient who processes information through words and numbers. Architect brother is a fun mixture of clairvoyance and intuition, so he gets clear, bottom-line "meaning" from the images he sees. Healer sister is also a mixture, her strengths being clairsentience and clairvoyance. If we weave this information with the idea of three brains—Head, Heart, and Gut[1]—there is even

---

1 The Head Feeling or reasoning brain observes the world, and is fueled by chemicals–allowing us to access words and create plans for the future; the Heart or feeling brain is the seat of our emotional intelligence allowing us to be in resonance with others and is based on electromagnetic fields. The electromagnetic field created by our heart is 100 times greater than our head brain. The Gut or knowing brain is our sensing or instinctive brain with fast processing of information is fueled by our gut microbes interacting with our cells. All three of these brains are connected by the vagus nerve and anything we can do to nourish the vagus nerve will help all three brains work better. http://yang-sheng.com/?p=10122

more depth to how we each show up with neurodiversity. Some of the conflicts between dad and sister, therefore, stemmed from their opposite ways of processing sensory information—Dad, through intellect, and my sister with a mostly visceral ("gut") reaction to life on earth. As a result, it was very hard for them to communicate and connect with each other, each feeling misunderstood and unappreciated by the other.

Maybe my choice of profession as a holistic doctor was an attempt to reconcile and integrate the influence of both parents. Certainly, it requires a life-long commitment and the expression of both art and science. As humans, we have right and left brains (as well as those in the gut and heart), and my goal is to be an integrated, whole-brain being to harmonize, align, and respect the wisdom of all my brains. As a result of that commitment, I generally follow the lead of my heart-brain. Using this inner GPS, I will "sense in" to the path with the greatest light, with the logic or rationale for that decision following later.

As mentioned, I live in a body that is sensitive and receptive to energies, so it was a blessing to be taught, at a young age, the value of time in nature, qi gong, and meditation as tools for processing the sensations and emotions that could flood my system. Imagine my surprise, when, after twenty years of mantra-based meditation, biofeedback revealed that what I had actually been practicing was the ability to dissociate. What I had thought was relaxation and meditation was not showing up as measurable positive physiological changes. Hmm…so how had I survived thousands of hours of emergency trauma work? Through willpower and mind-body dissociation—not a good recipe for long-term wellness and longevity. So, I had to learn more about body-based meditations, such as the observation of sensations, emotions, and thoughts, rather than escaping and avoiding. This self-regulation work was later supported by learning and consistently practicing body-mind-energy exercises that helped me connect with my body and keep my energy field clean and energy boundaries strong. I used qi gong practices that took seconds between patients and embraced more of a Taoist orientation towards meditation. This form has more of an emphasis on caring for the body (with the aim of longevity to support soul evolution), rather than a mental focus on escaping the body.

A subsequent step in living with greater joy as an empath involved intentionally creating healthy nervous system co-regulation with others. This work is brilliantly explained by Dr. Stephen Porges and the polyvagal theory. Our nervous systems are wired to be receptive to information emitted by other people's nervous systems. We can self-regulate and co-regulate our nervous systems in unhealthy and healthy ways. If you've ever wondered how coaching and mastermind groups facilitate growth, the answer is that we are tapping into the sage parts of others' nervous systems in healthy ways. I'd had plenty of experience with healthy self-regulation, having spent the first five decades of my life practicing that; however, it is only over the last ten years that I have focused on healthy co-regulation with others.

For example, as I navigate the care of elderly parents, I am clear that I am not just asking for help from others. I am being supported by "brains" that expand the capacity of my own nervous system. Engaging others' hearts, hands, and heads in creating a healthy neuro-network for my homestead is especially important as my parents are losing their mental and physical capacities. Much greater ease and grace as we travel with greater support.

As a doctor with expanded "soul senses" who has spent decades caring for others with similar gifts, here are some practices that keep me and those I care for living on purpose and expressing joy and freedom daily:

- Cultivating a strong observer that consciously and intentionally uses breath. Recognizing that sensations, emotions, and thoughts are transient, I claim my own alignment and center.

- Cultivating an awareness that sensations and emotions passing through our being are frequently not personal. Sometimes I am receptive to something happening somewhere else in the world. If I awaken out of sorts, I ask, "Is this mine?" When the answer is no, I say a prayer, do breathing and release work, and set clear alignment and intentions for the day.

- In the presence of others, I remind myself, "I do not know what you are feeling. I know only what I am feeling in your presence. I can only take responsibility for my own sensations, emotions, and thoughts."

- Meticulous, regular cleaning of the energy body. In addition to the material science taught in medical school, I've extensively studied Eastern medical traditions, which tell me that beyond my physical skin is an energy bubble and a membrane that I call my "second skin." Throughout my day I will practice sweeping (mentally and physically) and make sure I have enough movement and deep breathing to avoid energies getting stuck in my physical or energetic fields. Nighttime showers are also an important part of self-care.

- I find it useful to supplement my self-care practices with gems and minerals whether carried in my pocket or worn as jewelry—current favorites are turquoise and jade. Art, plants, and crystals in my work environment also help keep my space clean and clear.

- Honor body wisdom. Our body speaks in energy, not words. Our meridian systems, chakra systems, sacred geometry, and quantum physics are all woven into who we are as healthy, vibrant beings. Holding that knowing and being able to sit in silence, translate to words, song, dance, or art, is part of the joy of the human experience. I also use that body wisdom as part of my work—i.e. knowing where and how to touch another to help them come into balance.

- A cup of tea—the combination of its sight, smell, taste, and warmth—is one of my favorite medicines.

- Understanding that every day offers challenges to maintaining my balance and new resources for meeting those challenges.

These are just some of the tools that have been instrumental in helping me fulfill my life purpose, that of aligning and connecting with self and others in a way that serves a greater whole. My job is to use my sensitivities and my body to hold a space of higher frequency to be coherent and clear about the energy that is saturating and radiating from my nervous system's heart energy field. If I live in a constant state of overwhelm or suffering in resonance to what is happening in the world around me, I am of no service to anyone.

So, yes, I need regular time to decompress and defrag my system. This is not the lifetime to live in a cave, pray, and meditate. Living in balance is a dynamic dance; I know I will wobble, and that is okay. My learning journey involves the dance with alignment and connection with self and Source, the natural world, and others. Overall, the Tao of being an empath and the expression of spirit through body has been amazing and I am blessed and grateful for all the support the universe has provided.

ABOUT THE AUTHOR: Dr. Sharon Montes, MD, is an internationally recognized pioneer in the field of integrative health and holistic medicine. In her thirty-seven+ years of clinical experience, she has served as Medical Director for such prestigious health care facilities as The University of Maryland Center for Integrative Medicine; University of Colorado - Rose and AF Williams Family Medicine Centers; and North Texas Area Arlington Community Health Center. Committed to helping community leaders and compassionate warriors stay healthy, Dr. Montes continues to share her expertise as a lecturer, course director, and in radio and TV interviews. Currently, her primary focus is offering Living Well Resilience Programs to help others live with greater health, happiness, and efficiency.

Sharon Montes MD
livingwellwholehealth.com
livingwellhealthgroup.com

The Drain

You may spend your day cleaning up your house and office—perhaps you even clean up your language, thoughts, and interactions. What about consciously cleaning up your energy? This can be energy you choose to access with your thoughts and feelings, what you have picked up (often unconsciously) in your energy field, or energy that came in on your DNA. Whatever the source, your energy is with you all day, every day, affecting every second of your experience. It shows up at a job interview, at your cousin's wedding, and in your intimate relationship.

The Drain is an ultra-simple practice you can use anytime, anywhere, to clean up the energy you carry around. Now let's get started!

- Imagine a large drain in the floor below you, like in a shower. The cover of the drain has a one-way valve so energy only flows downward to empty into the void of creation; it also has adjustable holes that allow you to set the pace. Low vibrations are heavy and will easily flow down your drain. Positive vibrational energy stays high so it remains in your energy field.

- Picture an unseen flow of water from your magical energetic shower from Source pouring down.

- Now, ask any low vibrations or energy that is unbeneficial and negative to you to leave your body and energy fields and be washed down your drain.

- Ask to drain your physical energy field and notice what happens.

- Next, go down this list doing one at time: etheric, emotional, mental, ancestral, collective, planetary, galactic, Universal, and onward if you work with the expanded energies.

- Now it's time to fill yourself back up. This is a best practice when doing any energy work clearing, letting go, and cleaning to fill back up with energy you consciously request.

- Ask Absolute Love and Healing Golden Light from whatever source energy is for you to flow in your crown and fill up your entire body—cells, atoms, and space between your atoms—totally and completely.

You can put a drain anywhere you need one and at any time. Your drain will work automatically once installed.

CHAPTER 3

Inner GPS

Lu Stasko

Grand Purpose Seeker / Guiding People Simultaneously
Gentle Peaceful Spirit / Gathering Perfect Situations
Greater Powerful Sense / God's Plan Simplified
Go Plant Seeds

Most of us have heard of or know what GPS (Global Positioning System) is and how it is used to track the location of an entity or object remotely. It has become a tool most of us rely on every day. So, what is Inner GPS and how does it work? As you can see above, I have several other acronyms for it, but really they are all the same thing. It is that internal compass that appears in dreams, déjà vus, and knowings, providing spiritual guidance and helping us register a clear direction.

After college I worked for a Japanese company that exported beef from the United States. I was the only American and one of a few women who worked there. During my six years with this company, I learned a couple of good lessons: one, I do not like being an "employee," and two, I get bored easily. More importantly, I developed a way of circumventing the language barrier to understand and communicate with my superiors. We were even able to laugh together. It was a skill my boss used to say "would red carpet my future!" And he was right. This gift of "tuning in" and using my gifts of feeling the presence of my boss and co-workers really did open the doors to a brighter future for me.

Even though this was an excellent job right out of college, I knew in my heart that there had to be a better fit for me and my gifts and talents. And my Inner GPS would lead me there.

I started my career in publicity and public relations with no formal training or even an idea of what a publicist did. What I did have was a desire to help people, and a love of sharing their stories. I also had a "knowing" of who would enjoy hearing, and could benefit from, those stories. The early days of my company were trial-and-error. Since I didn't know what one did to get the attention of the journalists, news anchors, or other media outlets, I simply went on instinct, snail-mailing them my client's headshot, a brief overview of who they were, and a letter explaining their unique story or why people needed to hear about them or their business. I wasn't aware that I was providing "public relations" services until I mentioned it to a neighbor. He put a name to what I was doing and even gave me a news release so I could look more professional and "fit in" better in my chosen field.

Early on I received a call from the business editor of *The Denver Post*. When he asked how long I had been in the business, I hesitated; I assumed the method I was using was "wrong" and in fact was still doubting this new path. So, instead of answering his question directly, I asked, "Why do you ask?"

"Because," he replied, "You do this differently than everyone else. You have a unique approach in how you communicate with the media. You make our job easier."

As you can imagine I was surprised to hear this, and so grateful that I had trusted that inner GPS (Grand Purpose Seeker) to help me create a career path that would provide new opportunities every day and a situation in which I was my own employee. I was the boss of me, which seemed to please that inner guide.

Just as I didn't have the term or title for what I did, I had never known there was a name for my keen sense of knowing how to connect people to each other for purpose of business or life expansion and development. I never had a term that described the "knowing" that had guided me my entire life. As I explored this new definition, I gained a deeper understanding of many past dreams, nudges, feelings, and/or knowings, and a greater awareness of my inner GPS (Greater Powerful Sense). Indeed, I realized that being an empath had led me to my passion and purpose.

As a young girl, I was curious as to why sometimes things felt as though they had happened before. I recall in the fourth grade mentioning this to one of the nuns at my parochial school. She readily explained that what I was experiencing was called déjà vu; however, when I told her that these episodes seemed to be happening more often, she told me not to mention it again. I was simply to let these feelings pass, she said, and that is what I did.

Then the dreams started. Not every night, or every week, but from time to time I would dream about people or strange things. I remember vividly the dream that my aunt was going to be a grandma, which at the time seemed impossible because neither of her two kids was married or even in a relationship. When I called to tell her about my "funny" dream, I was shocked to hear her say, "I can't get anything by you." Her son, who was in his late teens, had had a one-night stand that resulted in a pregnancy! She has since become a grandma four times over, but that first grandchild was completely unexpected, and that dream had provided me with information I had no other way of accessing.

In time, I realized how tuned into others I am when I sleep or dream, receiving knowings about them out of the blue. I am always grateful when I can remember my dreams and am able to share the knowledge that has downloaded with the person, and I continued to be amazed how my Inner GPS (Gentle Peaceful Spirit) is always at work, even as I sleep.

This information also comes when I'm in a fully conscious state, often manifesting as a knowing, a feeling, or a physical unease that acts as a warning or in preparation for news, both pleasant and challenging. The most vivid knowing I had came when I was fourteen and about to go to a gymnastic meet in a town two hours from home. I woke up uneasy and reluctant about going, and though I pushed through the feeling it stayed with me through the day. I couldn't pinpoint the feeling, I just knew I would prefer to stay home and be close to my family that day. I remember counting down until we could leave, saying things like, "Two events done and six to go."

Finally, after what seemed like forever, my teammates and I piled into our coach's van. Before long, I realized that instead of passing my grandparents' ranch as she had on the way there, the coach was taking a different route. I believe this was an intuitive decision, and one I am very grateful for. When I got home, my dad met me at the front door with tears in his eyes. My grandpa and eighteen-year-old cousin were driving in a truck at the ranch when they were hit by a train. A "freak accident," he called it, which had taken my cousin's life. I knew that if my coach had taken the same route back I would have seen the site of that tragic accident. That knowing—that constant feeling—was real! It was the gift of being tuned-in and connected to a power greater than myself.

As the years went on these experiences—be they moments of déjà vu, dreams, or feelings of foreboding—became more familiar. I also became better at recognizing and listening to these spiritual nods, for which I am incredibly grateful, as it led me to build the company I've had for twenty-three years. During that time I have managed PR campaigns for developers, retailers, non-profits, government agencies, restaurants, associations, and marketing firms, and while my work has taken different shapes, directions, and designs, that Inner GPS, in one form or another, has been the most consistent, magical ingredient. For example, it is how I know to connect people to new media outlets and new target audiences; sometimes I even get a feeling about the timing to position an article in a well-read publication. It is instinctive and intuitive. This is my Inner GPS (Gathering Perfect Situations) at work.

There is a lot of information on empaths out there, but one of the most interesting tidbits is that they "remember too much." I choose to say that empaths have good memories—another skill that has served me very well! As mentioned, my career is based on connecting people, businesses, and communities—kind of like playing the game "Concentration" on a huge scale. For example, when meeting a new client I sometimes get a memory of something or someone that could assist them in their current endeavors. Time and time again, I have been able to put unlikely people or businesses together to create a perfect match—a result of trusting that inner GPS (Guiding People Simultaneously) to go to work for me and my clients.

I have also relied on other iterations of my Inner GPS throughout my career. For example, I often work with clients starting on the ground floor, helping them establish brand recognition in the market and then guiding them through expansions and further growth. As a result, Little Man Ice Cream became a must-see attraction in Denver's Lower Highland neighborhood and a well-known eatery is now on the map as one of the city's first sustainable restaurants. I also introduced out-of-state developers to new markets and helped them effectively navigate and address community concerns. The start-up companies I worked with have landed on Inc. 500's Fastest Growing Companies list and garnered investment and in some cases, buyers, because of the credibility we built in their industries through publicity, networking, and intuitive connection. This Inner GPS I refer to as "Growing Profit Shares."

Where my Inner GPS has really proved its importance, however, is in my personal life. The year 2020 was undoubtedly a challenging time for everyone; for me, it began with the passing of my mother. I was able to be by her side for a few days beforehand, and witness her relationship with her own Inner GPS, which showed up as physical changes. My mom, who was always quite beautiful, noticeably and increasingly glowed as her transition approached. Even others who came to see her commented on her glowing porcelain skin. It was a time of such peace and knowing, and one of the most beautiful moments I have ever experienced.

Within a few months of Mom's passing, I was faced with the challenge of my life when I heard those three words that strike fear in everyone's heart: "You have cancer." Yes, I was diagnosed with a very rare form of bone marrow cancer called Waldenstrom's macroglobulinemia. The first thought that came to my mind was, *This will soon be a distant memory. This too shall pass.* This Inner Knowing never left my thoughts as I spent most of the summer in the hospital, going through chemo, enduring nine rounds of plasmapheresis to cleanse my blood, extensive energy work, and nutritional refinement. I had no sooner been released from the hospital, after the most severe series of treatments, when my father also passed. It was just seven months after Mom died and five days before what would have been their sixty-second wedding anniversary. Their love was so strong, their connection so apparent, I knew it was supposed to be this way. Life has a funny way of mixing some obstacles in our paths that help us be more alert and listen to our Inner GPS more closely than ever before. I learned to trust that there is a reason for everything, and that the Inner GPS is one powerful source for all kinds of healing.

We are living in times that call for everyone to tune into their gifts—to not only find, but trust, their Inner GPS (God's Plan Simplified). I trust that by continuing to follow mine, my empathic gifts can only expand. I also trust that the déjà vus, the dreams, and knowings will all get a lot stronger as we come together in the collective and embrace the love and light God has always shone upon us. The clouds are lifting, and brightness is emerging. Be open—embrace the strong feelings you get to connect people, build something new, or create a new community. This is the time. I now know it was no mistake when I gathered a team of five brilliant men to develop a technology that allows GPS to work indoors. The company is called Prima Research, and today it holds four patents in the Indoor Location-Based industry, all because I listened to my Inner GPS (Go Plant Seeds)!

ABOUT THE AUTHOR: Lu Stasko is a master relationship builder. She established her public relations and marketing firm, The Stasko Agency, to connect entrepreneurs with the resources and audiences needed to help them succeed and grow. Through her powerful network of media contacts, policy makers, and community leaders, Lu has helped clients attract investors, achieve revenue goals, and gain public approval for crucial projects. Her diverse client list includes real estate developers, restaurants, local municipalities, technology startups, nonprofits, retailers, and business associations. Lu also supports a number of nonprofits, serves as an advocate for her North Denver neighborhood, and enjoys consulting with small town communities in refreshing their marketing and business strategies.

Lu Stasko
The Stasko Agency
lu@staskoagency.com
staskoagency.com

EMPATH TOOL
by Jade Rehder

Sovereign-Self Sourcing

As an empath, you naturally and magnetically attract energy, emotions, feelings, pain, thoughts, information, knowing, people, experiences, and more into your multidimensional physical, emotional, mental, and spiritual energy fields. When you are unaware that you're receiving, the effect of energies coming "at" you is even stronger. The following practice provides protection by connection, and is the most powerful I have found for empaths. Using the metaphor of a radio station, it allows you to adjust these frequencies and stop overwhelm and anxiety. You can also use that receiver to consciously attract your Sovereign-Self wisdom and Source energy!

Doing this practice consciously and daily will allow you to more easily experience life.

- Sit down and close your eyes.

- Allow yourself to experience that you are sending a pillar of energy/light from your root center down until it connects to your Earth Star, 12 to 18 inches below the Earth's surface.

- Notice that you are connected and grounded.

- Continue sending the energy pillar into the Earth's center, connecting with the diamond core or whatever appears for you.

- Now send the energy pillar to your star/spark origin, or Source Light. (There is no need to know its name)

- From your Source Light, send the energy back to the Earth plane to your Soul Star/High self.

- Next, send the energy/light from your Soul/Sol Star through your body.

- Notice your Crown, Heart, and Root centers on the way to your Earth Star.

- Allow the light, wisdom, and energy to flow back and forth freely, filling you with energy and light from the inside.

- Run the circuit of energy a second time, enhancing the strength flow from your Root to Earth Star, Earth center, Source Light, Soul/Sol Star, Crown, Heart to Root.

- Now, reverse the connection, from your Root, Heart, Crown, Soul Star, Source Light to your Earth center, Earth Star, and Root. Then repeat the process one more time, for a total of four loops, coming a little further and ending in your heart center.

- Now the magic happens! State: "In the name of the Light, my centers are tuned to receive from my field of wisdom and Light."

- Silently or aloud, count down, asking your centers 12 to 1 to attract and receive from the inside 360 degrees toward your spine, where the stream of your Soul/Sol Energy is flowing filled with your wisdom, high consciousness, and Source information.

- Ask to anchor, establish, and maintain this connection.

CHAPTER 4

The Power of Leaning In

How Curiosity and Trusting My Intuition
Helped Me Find My Calling

Tiffany Espinosa

When my mom found out she was going to have a baby, she thought it was an April Fool's joke. She had long accepted what doctors told her—that she would never have children—and now, at thirty-five years old, she was not only pregnant but six months along! Always fiercely independent, Mom was in her prime, and in the habit of leaning into life on her own terms. Then everything changed. Eight weeks after receiving the news, she went into labor and I slipped into the world a scrawny, curious baby.

My birth represented a complete plot twist for my mom. Believing motherhood wasn't in the cards, she had never spent an iota of her energy thinking about what kind of parent she wanted to be, or what kind of a child she hoped to have. This gave me room to grow into my own person; I was never pressured to live up to any idealized versions she had created in her mind.

We were both lucky that she didn't have strong opinions about how I should be. While not loud or pushy, I've always had a strong spirit. With my roots deeply grounded, and a strong sense of my own true north, I have been an indomitable force. It is what has allowed me to take punches, pick myself up, and jump right back in the ring to fight for what I believe in.

From the earliest time I can remember, I have been very tender to the pain of the world. The suffering of people half a world away can create an aching grief that I feel in the deepest parts of my heart. Gashes in the earth, clearcut forests, the lost and abandoned—they all strike a nerve deep within me because I know we are all connected. The twin flames of a strong and sensitive spirit has been fuel for me, but I had to learn early on how to turn down the flow lest I be carried off by the current. Even today tapping into it can feel overwhelming and I am still learning to walk the tightrope between the vulnerability of openness and withdrawal.

Growing up, I spent more time around adults than I did kids my own age. Mom's salary didn't really include enough for a babysitter, so I was her constant little companion and often engaged with her peers. The benefit of being a quiet kid in adult spaces is that you become invisible. People are more authentic, more raw, when they don't realize they are being observed.

Watching, but unseen, I had a wonderful vantage point. It is where I started to build my empathy and map the complicated geographies of the inner worlds of the people around me. I watched adults navigate profound sadness and deep depression while also being alive with joy and passion. I watched successful, well-loved people plagued with anxiety. I learned the world was often "both/and," with layers of feelings, thoughts, attitudes, and beliefs that connected in paradoxical ways, like M. C. Escher's maps of impossible spaces. The complexity has always fascinated me and stoked my curiosity. I lean into these interior worlds, exploring how gravity and physics work according to people's individual cosmologies. And while there are patterns, each person is a beautiful and unique universe, knit together from what is particular to them.

Having been raised in a world of adults, I didn't fit in well with kids. I didn't understand them and I didn't know how to engage with them, so mostly I went unnoticed. Again, being invisible gave me the space to grow on my own terms and develop my sensitivities and sensibilities. My curiosity, a driving force and one of my superpowers, helped me become even more attuned to the world around me. Being sensitive and curious have worked together as a flywheel in my life, propelling me forward and generating energy both for me and that emanates from me. It is also at the heart of my empathic gifts.

Understanding what it means to be invisible has led me to be more sensitive to what it means to be seen and vulnerable. Being attuned to the flow of energy when I am working with people has given me an ability to hold them tenderly. A lot of people I encounter are not used to being really seen. In a world full of transactional exchanges, it is less common to have someone show up and be fully present, listening both to what you are saying and what you aren't saying, and to gently encourage you to take the risks. Being seen means you are able to share what is tender and most precious to you, and to trust that you are safe. It is proof that you are alive, and your truths matter, and someone is bearing witness. For most, it is both empowering and a bit terrifying. Being present for people is about creating space for them to bring their full selves, paradoxes and all. People being seen make eye contact and heart contact in a very different way; at first it can be timidly, but then they relax into it and learn they can be authentic, vulnerable, messy, and loved, all at the same time. It doesn't have to make sense or be linear. I have learned how to hear the quiet call of other hearts and to gently hold them while they grow more confident in themselves and strong.

My empathy helps me midwife people through transitions. For over twenty-five years, both professionally and as a volunteer, I have mentored adults and youth as they prepare for and move to new stages in their lives. I hold up mirrors as they look into their hearts to find what animates their souls. I sit shiva with them as they mourn what is passing away. I provide a steady hand and encouragement as they learn to walk in new territories. I offer them grace until they can give it to themselves.

Since I'm not wired to measure myself based on the approval of others, it's easier to be authentic, honest, and maintain my personal boundaries when I am working with people. I can hold space for their fears and anxieties, creating the opportunity for them to stretch and grow. I can see what is possible in them before they are able to see it or believe in it themselves. I help them orient their maps and learn how to use their own gears and levers to generate energy and momentum. As I lead our dance between exploring the world as it is and what else is possible, they start to find their own rhythm. My gifts help me discern and attend to the pastoral needs of the people I work with as they grapple with the edges of their learning curves. I wasn't trained how to see and hold people through transition; rather, it has been an instinctual, spiritual expression. That said, I have worked on honing it as I've gotten older.

My journey has not been without challenges, one being that it took me many years to become aware of and learn to honor my intuition. Taught to believe in the primacy of cognition, I didn't have a framework for it. Because intuition operates outside the realm of language, logic, and evidence, it felt ephemeral and clandestine to me. This made it more difficult for me to process what it means and how to use it in my life.

I remember stumbling across the concept of "presencing" a decade ago and feeling like I finally had words for my experience and how it was manifesting in my life. Arising out of a vision for how we can co-create the future and hold space for one another, it is centered in diving deep together, listening, holding the areas of tensions, and staying connected. The concept was incubated in the world of organizational change, but has much wider applicability to supporting personal and social transformation as well. It was like coming home.

I experience presencing as the embodiment of my intuition as

I engage with the world. It is a rebel knowledge, refusing to be bound by language or logic. Strong and sometimes unruly, it has nevertheless always been on target for me. It doesn't always feel like flow, or certainty. It doesn't always lead to easy times or comfortable experiences. It is like a live wire, plugged directly into my heart. It can feel like a glow, a warmth, an itch, uneasiness, or insistent tugging. It is a constant companion. It took years of feeling it, and experimenting with letting it lead me, before I began to be able to interpret the subtle signals that arose from it in my body and energy. I'm still a work in progress, but as my fluency has grown, so has the strength of this gift.

If my intuition helped me find my calling, curiosity is how I have leaned into my path. It took me a long time to really understand its role and power and, in retrospect, it is clear that it was the engine behind so much of what I do. My curiosity has led me to passions, drove me to build my expertise, and helped me connect with people from a place of authenticity and enthusiasm.

The beauty of curiosity is that it can be learned and mindfully cultivated. While it came very naturally to me, I also feed this taproot regularly. Curiosity is a critical component in establishing understanding and trust between people. Probing the edges of what we know and how we know it, we become seekers. We build better, more multidimensional maps to guide us. It bolsters our dexterity and the path becomes easier.

I develop my curiosity by trying new things, even if I'm not very good at them. I explore the world around me; I travel and allow myself to get lost. I ask a lot of questions. I celebrate failure as a signal of trying something new and learning in the process. I read a lot, across disciplines and genres. I talk to strangers. I regularly ask myself what else is possible and how can it be better than this. I brainstorm. I learn new words. I jump at every chance to be creative. I have earned degrees in social science, business, education, and natural resources. I look for new problems to understand. I teach— which ironically is a wonderful way to learn, because if you give students the space they will always show you a new way to see and think about the topic you are investigating together. I work with entrepreneurs and community catalysts. I hang out with kids and ask questions with them. Leaning into curiosity has helped me see common threads and new patterns. I find it stimulating and exhilarating, and more often than not it has been a source of finding kinship with others. I've learned to invite people on adventures and I've always found ready companions.

Over the years my curiosity has helped me build my expertise and develop my gifts, and, importantly, it has also helped me find community. Community has been critical to help buoy me when my connection to the pain of the world becomes too much. It has been where I find validation and where I have come to understand my gifts and how to use them. It is through my community that I see myself reflected in a mosaic of mirrors. A critical milestone in my personal development was learning how to name and channel my empathy so it could enhance my relationships.

Another challenge has been balancing that connection with the solitude I need to stay centered. Indeed, it is a delicate art to be fully present and focused on the people I care the most deeply about while also keeping my own needs and desires at the table. Being so sensitive to the world, it can be easy to lose sight of myself, honor what I need and get support. I'm learning to be more mindful about attending to myself.

It has also been important for me to learn to articulate my capacities and internal experiences so that I am better able to nurture and support them. It has been a lot like my experience as a young athlete. Until my athleticism and natural competitive streak were channeled into sports, I didn't know the power and beauty of my body or what I could be capable of. I ended up being a four-sport athlete with very discrete gifts that my coaches were able to see and help me polish. If you don't know what you are trying to develop, it's very difficult to find the right coaches.

Learning how to survive in the world has not always been easy. As I have developed a better framework and language for who I am and what I bring to others, I can seek out mentors and guides. This, in turn, has made me a better coach for people who are struggling to fully grasp and trust their own natural gifts. My gifts have become my offerings, and my offerings have become ways that I connect, thrive, and evolve.

ABOUT THE AUTHOR: Dr. Tiffany Espinosa is a social entrepreneur who helps individuals and organizations level up. Since 2017 she has been the executive director of professional and graduate education for Mount Holyoke College. She is an executive business coach for the Goldman Sachs 10,000 Small Businesses Program and leads Teal Executives, a business strategy and executive coaching firm. She serves as a board member for Girls Inc. of the Valley and volunteers with EForAll Holyoke and She Leads, an initiative of the Easthampton Chamber of Commerce. She believes in the power of empowered, inspired people and collaboration.

Tiffany Espinosa
Teal Executives
tealexecutives.com
tespinosa@tealexecutives.com
linkedin.com/in/tiffanyespinosa

EMPATH TOOL
by Jade Rehder

WHAT IF. . .Spiral Up

When an empath is in a highly charged or traumatic experience, it's easy to go into a loop of self-questioning that quickly spirals downward into the torment of self-criticism and self-doubt. (This can look like Chicken Little's famous rant). WHAT IF you chose to turn the energetic momentum around and started to spiral it up instead?

Say the following out loud:

What If there are different possibilities?

What If all the people in the situation contributed to the optimal result?

What If you can find something to learn from the situation?

What If you could sit in the stream of curiosity?

What If you could wonder with an open mind?

What If _____?

What If _____?

What If _____?

What if things could turn out better than you could ever imagine?

What If the field of wonder brings you a new perspective?

What If thing get better and better?

You can use this practice whenever you find yourself in a challenging situation or if you get up in the morning feeling off. Doing a WHAT IF Spiral Up helps you tap into your natural curiosity and wonder and open the flow for your day!

CHAPTER 5

Fully Human

The Walk of an Empath

Serin N. Silva

I spent a big part of my life unconscious of my true nature. Growing up, I heard a lot of "toos" from my parents, relatives, and other adults—I was "too sensitive"; "too upset "; "too passionate." This may be an odd analogy, but if I was to compare myself back then to a machine, it would have been a big, seventies-style block of metal with two giant switches marked "'Sob" and "Scream." There were no other options to push.

Honestly, I just figured something was wrong with me, and there was never a shortage of people around to validate that. In my career, I would hear, "Why do you always have to swing for the fences?" because I poured so much passion into the ideas I cared about. Even my name, given to me by my Turkish-Cypriot parents, was different-sounding than most; in fact, Serin was not a "normal" Turkish name either. In my mind, I was just one big package of Weird, and oftentimes found myself close to pressing those "sob" and "scream" switches.

I functioned in my hyper-conformist world and looked for the in-between times. When I was alone, I could let go of all the "toos" and just dream. I'd turn out the lights in my small bedroom to quiet the space, look out the window, stare at the stars, and ask for answers. Sometimes, I'd feel a response—a lightness in my body, an opening of my heart, a greater appreciation of the night sky. I always felt better when I took the time to commune with myself in this way. It was, and still is, a wonderful respite.

I never heard the terms "intuitive" or "empath" until I was about forty. That was also the time when my husband said to me, "I think you're psychic and you should take a class." I'm afraid I raked him over the coals for that one! I thought it was a ridiculous notion and, quite frankly, a bit insulting. Undeterred, he went on to tell me about my precognition, potential channeling abilities, and so on. He was a computer engineer at the time, so it seemed even sillier to hear it fall out of his mouth. Still, I had to admit my curiosity was piqued, though I did keep looking for the hidden camera.

I found myself in Big Sur, California for a Gestalt weekend and was paired with a lean Israeli man around the same age. We learned we shared similar childhood stories, and that it was easy for us to exchange energy via our hands—without touching. I remember the sun filling up the wood-paneled room as he and I laughed and moved further and further apart to see if we could still pass energy. We could. I wasn't sure what this was, all I knew is that I didn't feel "too" anything and I didn't feel Weird. It felt very natural, like "home," and I just wanted to keep doing it. I was like a kid who had stumbled onto a new world and though I still questioned whether I should trust my experience, it was just so damn fun.

From there, things just got more dynamic and curious as I settled into my Otherness, and the fact that I had this ability. Then, in July of 2005 I flew to London for work and found I felt extremely unsettled—odd, since I had family in the UK and had been traveling there since I was eight months old.

I was in a nice hotel in a safe neighborhood, yet I just laid in the bed unable to stop crying, an inexplicable anxiety, bordering on panic, deep in my bones. It was as if someone had told me my dog died or that I'd lost a family member. When I called my husband and tried to put what I was feeling into words, he was, understandably, very concerned. I left my work meetings early, headed back on the London Underground Express train to Heathrow and jumped on a plane to D.C., still completely confused as to why I was so weepy and needed to go home. Again, this was very unlike me—an experienced traveler who felt at home on planes and loved to roam and explore new cities.

As I was walking through the D.C. airport, I distinctly remember looking at the TV monitor and seeing the headline "Coordinated suicide bomb attacks on the London transit system." An explosion had torn through three trains on the London Underground, killing thirty-nine people and injuring a total of seven hundred. Astounded, I knew without a doubt that this event was connected to the anxiety I had been feeling. Still, I couldn't quite put a name to what had happened until someone told me, "You're an empath."

From that point forward, I began to look at myself differently. I felt less Weird, and more special, to be honest. Maybe all of my non-conformity was there for an actual reason. Maybe I wasn't broken. Maybe it was okay that I didn't fit the mold. Maybe there was actually nothing wrong with me. Maybe I had been granted gifts. Maybe there was another world, another place, another cosmos, another energy. Maybe it was time to drop it and stop trying to fit in and look beyond the day-to-day routine. Maybe, just maybe, there was a damn good reason I had been given these gifts, and I was determined to find out what it was.

That kicked off a Googling extravaganza. An avid learner, my solution to everything has always been to read and learn my way through. Surely I could find documented research around what this was, get all my answers, find my group, and be oh-so-validated. Well, yes and no. I did find some information and community, but nothing specific enough to my experience—i.e. "You're in London and you need to leave real quick because there's an attack coming." At some point, I gave up looking for The Answer because I realized it was more about justifying my existence and telling people I was not Weird—and that is so *not* the point. I can feel the laughter in the air from spirit guides, Source, and the planet as I type this. Being liked, loved, and validated are human constructs—nothing more. They feed the human ego. Now, there's nothing wrong with taking care of my egoic needs, per se, but it is not why I am an empath.

I realized this is in me, developing, and doing its thing; whatever it is or is supposed to be doesn't matter. It is not part of my prescribed human world, but beyond that, and to name it, describe it, and label it has nothing to do with why I am an empath. I just am...like the sun in the sky, the stars in the night, the water in the sea, and the flowering of the trees.

My empathic nature is so beautiful and cherished within me now. It is my home and what I believe makes me a full human—three hundred and sixty degrees of yumminess, connectivity, intuition, community, and insight. I feel all of my feelings—like digesting a rich, gourmet plate of food, I get to savor and feel everything. And yes, it can be overwhelming, but I wouldn't have it any other way.

Now, there are downsides, challenges, or things to watch out for. Part of why I am sharing this story is because I don't want people to have to hunt and peck their way through as I did. Yes, it can be fun to learn new things, but not when we're talking about things that can be super-draining, sometimes scary, and downright confusing. Best to be prepared, share with others, and invite other empaths into the fold.

Before Discovering I was an Empath

As an extrovert, I would move through the world as if I was trying to take a bite out of it. I would just bring my full self into any conversation and with anyone. One time, I was at the grocery store and said hello to the checkout person. She met my smile and began to tell me the story of her cancer treatment in our minutes-long interaction. I could feel her pain, sadness, and fear and offered up good thoughts and a message of speedy healing. I remember going home that day and feeling sad. It was days later that I realized I was picking up her energy by giving myself fully to our conversation. The sadness was her sadness, not mine. I wasn't the one with cancer.

I don't think I knew that I needed to contain my energy. I'm an extroverted, friendly, curious type and so I would enjoy the ride of these interactions. I always allowed my energy to just spill forward to whomever I met, without thinking about the fact that I was an energetic sponge. It sounds very human and honorable to be there to witness another person's experience, but the endless contact, without space to remove or offload, would make me super-moody, tired, and sick. My mind would be very interested, engaged, and happy for the connection, but my energy was a totally different story. At first I thought I had an illness and went to a bunch of doctors. That wasn't the cause of the exhaustion, I later found.

After Discovering I was an Empath

I'm still happy to meet people—they are an endless curiosity for me and I like human connection. That said, I've learned that I need to have more energetic hygiene when connecting to others, particularly as an intuitive medium and coach.

Everyday Energy Hygiene

Like washing my hair, I proactively manage my energy boundaries. I call it hygiene, except I can't see it like I can with shampoo lather. It needs to be done before, during, and after interactions with others.

In my healing work, I started with better beginning and ending processes. I used a singing bowl to set the space, deep breathing, and then let the participant know that we were working together at this point in time for the purpose of healing. At the end of the session, I would remind the participant (and myself) that when our connection was closed, we would no longer be connected. In my mediumship work, it's particularly important because after I drop a connection, people's loved ones can sometimes hang around energetically. If I don't have good energy boundaries I feel icky, and if not managed it can lead to illness.

Understanding My Limits

Limits aren't just for knowing when I should stop drinking or when I should go to bed. There are also limits to my energy boundary and capacity. It took time to learn that I needed to slow down, be present, breathe, and not chase stimuli so much.

My mind would often press me along to get to the next thing, meet the next person, and push myself hard to achieve my real-world goals. While there is nothing wrong with being self-motivated, there are energy limits to what I can expose myself to. I had to start noticing before and after, was this a draining interaction or an uplifting one? I noted these in my calendar.

Letting Go of What's Not Mine

After an intense interaction, I step back and look at what energy was mine and what was theirs and why. Do I want to have another interaction with this person, or is it best that I don't meet with them again? If I didn't have a choice in the matter, I would then go into energy hygiene before my next interaction and set an intention for our meeting. Intention-setting for me is not making a wish, but understanding why I am choosing something and how I might like the outcome to be.

Being an empath is like breathing. And when I breathe, I don't hold onto the air, I release it. This is a good reminder to not hold onto the dynamics and energy of what happens here. I'm a breathing, living force, here to feel my full humanness. I do so with gratitude. It is truly a gift to be an empath walking on Mother's Earth. I can't imagine living any other way.

ABOUT THE AUTHOR: Serin Silva is a beloved medium, intuitive healer, instinct coach, and founder of Kismet Energies. After becoming disenchanted with humanity's disconnection from its evolutionary roots, Serin turned to information locked within herself for answers. For Serin, life is beyond what we think. It is about accessing innate information humans have long left behind in the pursuit of progress. Serin teaches people to harness their instincts and to be truly at home with themselves. By accessing individual needs and desires, we can live in true harmony with ourselves and our greater world. Connect with Serin and learn more about her work at kismetenergies.com

Serin N. Silva
Kismet Energies
kismetenergies.com
serin@serinsilva.com

Balance Breath

Have you ever asked yourself how you can turn things around when you are feeling totally unbalanced or overwhelmed? You know, the times when you walk into the next room and can't remember why you are there, or you get to the store and forget the most important item you meant to purchase. Or the days when you get to work and realize that your body feels heavy—your energy feels dull and stuck—and you are completely unmotivated! Or any time when so much is happening that you come to a standstill, paralyzed, and unable to begin anything at all.

When you practice the Balance Breath, you move, increase, and expand the amount of air flowing in your body and mind. The result? You feel lighter, mentally clearer, less stuck, and more balanced. Balance breath works quickly and you can use it anywhere.

ASKercise the Balance Breath

- Breathe in through your nose, slowly, for a count of four.

- Breathe out through your mouth, slowly, making an *ahhh* sound for a count of four. (This is a 1-to-1 ratio.)

- Do a set of this harmonious in/out breath (four times).

- Check in with your body and feel if you feel lighter and your energy is more equalized throughout. You may feel as if you can move more freely.

- Does your mind still feel cluttered? Does it feel easier to focus on a specific thought?

- If you're still feeling stuck or mind-cluttered, do another set of four slow in/out breaths.

To take the practice further, picture the pores of your skin (your largest organ) opening wide as you bring air in through them. You will quickly feel much lighter. Doing this is a great way to release stress and become aware of energy blockages. Focus on where the energy is stuck, feel it in your body, perhaps between your shoulders or in your lower back. If it feels right, lay down on your back on the floor and bend your knees. Breathe the Balanced Breath, focusing on the area where you feel the tightness, and notice as it dissipates. You may find it happens quickly.

Let Go Breath

The Let Go Breath is an effective way to quickly calm the mind and body. It came to me via my training in Ancient Hawaiian Huna, where it is called the HA Breath. The breath of life. I have used it in heavy traffic, when I have a challenging schedule, and even when I disagree with someone's point of view. I know I create my own reality and that respecting the other person's model of the world is part of the journey. The Let Go Breath helps me stay centered in my own truth while remaining respectful of the other person and open to other points of view. I encourage you to use this simple practice often when you want to get in your body, *let go,* and be at peace.

Let Go Breath

- Breathe in through your nose for the count of four thinking *let*.

- Breathe out through your mouth for the count of eight thinking *go*.

- Slightly restrict the back of your throat creating a "ha" sound, very much like the gentle movement of the ocean,

- Do this four times, and then breathe normally for a few breaths.

- Repeat three more times for a total of four sets of four.

You feel calmer and centered now, right?

CHAPTER 6

This Life Is a Gift
Christina Sloan

One of my very first memories is of being on the playground of the elementary school right behind our home. There was an old-fashioned tire swing—you know, one of the flat ones with the three chains on it. As I was laying on that tire swing, my legs too short to touch the ground, I looked up at the beautiful, clear summer sky and had this overwhelming feeling of the vastness of the world. I was five years old.

That moment has always stuck with me because it was so intense and involved such a mature thought process for one so young. I clearly recall contemplating the meaning of life, and wondering why I was here, in this family, this place in the world, and at this time. I remember feeling so present and so expansive, and thinking to my five-year-old self, *This life is a gift.* I also had a knowing inside myself that I had special gifts and a tremendous opportunity to share them with the world.

I even knew, as I was spinning around on that tire swing, that this was a really important moment in my life, a realization that brought tears streaming from my eyes. I stayed there for probably an hour or more, then walked back to my house, thinking—no, *knowing*—that I would never be the same.

Today, forty years and countless life lessons later, I can see that the experience was wholly in tune and connected with universal consciousness. Though I was instinctively aware of the importance of stepping into my gifts, it would take more than three decades before I really started to understand what it meant to be a highly sensitive person, a powerful manifester, and an empath.

Over the course of this journey, memories from my childhood have been omnipresent, guiding me and helping me understand who I truly was before I was shaped by my family, schools, and society in general. Super-intense and highly sensitive, I felt everything and everyone around me, which made it really hard to be around others. This, coupled with fierce independence and a really unhealthy lack of fear, led me to spend a lot of time alone and off on my own adventures.

My mom loves to tell the story of the day I went missing from my crib. I was two-and-a-half years old, and after putting me down for a nap she had gone to rest herself while my father and brothers did yard work. When she woke up and saw my crib was empty, she asked my father where I was. He didn't know, and panic and chaos ensued until the next-door neighbor pulled up, jokingly asked my parents if they were missing anyone, and then helped me out of their car. Apparently, after escaping the confines of my crib I had wandered off into the woods behind our house. The neighbor had found me walking along the side of the New Jersey Turnpike—a mile or so away!

To me, this is so telling about who I was authentically as a child. I felt so held and protected, like nothing could harm me. I trusted my gut instincts and was led by intuition; I was curious, adventurous, and free-spirited. Over time, however, this was figuratively beaten out of me as I was shaped, indoctrinated into societal norms and, at eighteen, reluctantly led to our floundering third-generation family business.

I soon found myself juggling college classes and the colossal task of re-growing this business with my two older brothers. I had to step into a leadership role very quickly, with very little leadership experience and often managing men twice my age who didn't respect me. Initially, my instincts were to suppress my sensitivities and for the first couple of years this worked to some degree. I found I was natural in business—a very strategic and creative thinker, action-oriented, organized, and driven. I also earned the respect of my employees and we had a lot of growth and success.

Ultimately though, I felt disconnected from those around me, and they felt it too. My confidence started to erode under the weight of the constant stress and responsibility for the livelihood of so many people. When I started getting physically sick, I realized I had to stop stretching myself beyond who I really was at my core. Being raised in a family of entrepreneurs, I had been told from a very young age that "there is no crying in business," and "business isn't personal." I remember thinking, *Screw it! I am who I am, and being a highly sensitive, deeply feeling person in business can't be wrong.* I understood that businesses are made up of human beings with souls, and there is no way we can separate who we are at work from who we are in life. People need a deeper connection with and a higher level of purpose in their work. These thoughts would develop into a central theme in my career.

From that point on, I started leaning into my sensitivities instead of trying to run from them. Soon I was connecting more deeply with the people around me; I could feel them again, and could feel myself moving with them energetically, like a dance. Work became fulfilling for me and for the employees in my care. I could sense what they needed, and they felt trusted and integral to our success. Moreover, as they thrived within in our organization, the way they showed up in their families and communities changed. This realization increased my sense of purpose as well. Suddenly, we weren't in business just to produce and sell our products, we were in business to change lives for the better.

Ultimately, this led to our continual success and growth because we were all in this thing together—caring about each other and the work we were doing. I got to see the cycle of true fulfillment, where people are living into their gifts and being who they are authentically. For me, it was confirmation that my sensitivities were actually strengths. It was about trusting that being an empath is who I am and what I am is meant to be shared with the world.

Eventually, we sold our family business and I went on to work for other leaders and organizations. For the first time I got to see how the traditional business world worked and—what a learning opportunity this was for me. I became so passionate about how business should and could be done differently that it shaped my career path. It led me to organizational development, people operations, leadership development, and conscious leadership.

Along the way I worked with some really challenging and very unhealthy leaders, and I also worked with some phenomenal self-aware, conscious leaders—including other empaths. I was immediately drawn to these individuals, as they broadened my thinking even more. Some became great mentors to me, while others challenged and inspired me to grow even beyond where I could have imagined possible.

In March of 2020, one of my mentors told me, "Christina, you are playing small. You have so much more to give to the world." Though this statement would have given me pause under any circumstances, it was especially meaningful because of the timing. While I was very happy and content leading a mid-market company, I had also started to feel the tug of something more. The next week, her words would seem absolutely precognizant. Our industry was shut down by COVID, and the world changed overnight. My path changed as well, and I found myself leaving a job I'd thought I'd be in for the rest of my career.

I decided then that I was going to go out on my own and start my own company. I didn't know what this would look like, or how I would support myself. I also knew, on an intellectual level, that it was crazy to leave a six-figure income (especially since I was newly single), with no real plan and no income stream in sight. Yet, I wasn't afraid; in fact, for the first time since I was that free-spirited, adventurous child I felt truly held and supported by the Universe. I felt grounded and very present. For the next few months, I just took time to take care of me. I hiked in nature, I journaled, and I meditated. I also focused on nurturing the skill sets that I have as an empath—my intuition and sensitivities—as well as all the training I've had around conscious leadership. I just took all of that and sat with it, while also having fun, traveling, and reconnecting with and nurturing my close relationships. Before long, things started to come to me in the form of ideas and inspired action.

Those ideas made sense and felt right for me in my body. I was manifesting and visualizing my future life, watching and noticing the synchronicities and signs all around me, and allowing them to guide me. I just knew with one hundred percent confidence that everything would work out the way it was supposed to, and I didn't put any energy into worrying. Every single month since starting my business I've earned enough money to support myself; I'm also doing really meaningful work—more meaningful than my logical brain could have come up with in a strategic planning session or by sitting down and trying to think my way through a business plan. I am intuitively aware that I am at the precipice of the next chapter of my life, a life where for the first time I am fully empowered and enabled to authentically live into my innate strengths and gifts. Although I am a powerful strategic thinker and naturally gifted as an operational integrator, these qualities feel very rooted in my masculine energy. This new chapter feels much more balanced in both the masculine and feminine.

Being a highly sensitive being and empath, combined with my training as a conscious leader and all the twists and turns of my career over the last twenty-five years, has given me the ability to help companies and organizations elevate more consciously, and leaders to align their personal and professional lives with their purpose and personal values. This is my calling, and the answer to the questions I asked myself on the tire swing that day. It is why I am here at this time, in this place, and was born to this family.

Recently, I was struck by the realization that I am more like that five-year-old now than I have been at any point since that day. That little girl was wise far beyond her years, and I have learned to embrace and cherish her. As empaths, it is so important that we nurture these gifts and listen to our intuition, allowing it to guide us. It doesn't matter how old we are chronologically; we have an extra intelligence that we were born with and for a reason, a higher purpose. Some of us are healers or magic-makers, and some of us are visionaries, way-showers, and trailblazers. The latter are the people who create new paths and norms for how we do things in society, to help elevate the collective consciousness. It is no accident that more and more people are waking up to this at this particular time in human history. It is our duty and our calling to lean into our innate gifts, rather than suppressing them to more easily fit into societal norms; nor can we stay comfortably on the fringe of society any longer. We need to realize that we don't fit in, because we're not supposed to. We have too much to offer the world.

ABOUT THE AUTHOR: Christina Sloan is a conscious leader, visionary, and integrator with a passion for operationalizing growth strategies in purpose-driven, people-centric, conscious business environments. With more than two decades of diverse experience as an entrepreneur, C-level executive, and consultant, she founded Transcending U, providing consulting, coaching, training, and leadership development within organizational development to maximize profits while building an empowering culture. Christina is a founding board member of Conscious Capitalism Kansas City, and a certified Conscious Leader and Shakti Leadership Fellow through the University of San Diego Conscious Leadership Academy. She is based in Kansas City and loves being outdoors, traveling, and spending meaningful time with friends and family.

Christina Sloan, Founder, Visionary & Integrator
Transcending U
transcendingu.com
christina@transcendingu.com
816-519-6881

EMPATH TOOL
by Jade Rehder

Ring of Knowing

You can do this with any way of feeling you would like to increase the amount of power you have behind the energy.

Create a list of what you feel are your knowing words, phrases, feelings, emotions, sounds, and songs. Recall events and places where you felt your self-worth, self-love, seen and heard at a high level, and the strongest belief that these energies support your inner knowing.

- Imagine a circle in front of you. It can be any size you like; it can be solid or multiple colors. You can also use a visual prop (I have used a hula-hoop). This is your Ring of Knowing.

- Now, visualize the places and experiences where your powerful knowing has shown up in your life; put them inside your Ring of Knowing.

- Add your knowing songs and sounds to the Ring. What phrases are you saying to yourself when you are feeling your self-worth and self-love intensely? Remember your personal sound. This is a knowing sound for you.

- Next, add your personal Ring of Knowing feelings and emotions: self-love, the self-knowing of being seen, the love you feel when you are heard by yourself and others, and whatever else is on your list or comes to mind to create the feeling of Knowing your worth.

- Now, step into the ring.

- Feel the flow of self-worth, knowing, and self-love wash into you.

- Imagine everything you have energized your Ring of Knowing with covering you like a layer of energetic love.

- Invite the energy of Knowing to be preserved in an active state, being the vibe that is playing in the background supporting you.

You can add more to your Ring of Knowing anytime you choose.

When you have visualized and actively experienced your Ring of Knowing a few times and are connected to it at a deep level, you will need only to imagine it and all the resources will come to you in an instant! "Ring of Knowing ACTIVE!" Just like a superhero puts on their tights and cape, you have yours. It's invisible and no cape is needed, unless of course you want one!

CHAPTER 7

The Spaces In Between

Roses, Tangerines, and Miracles...

Monica Jaramillo

My mom and dad had a busy social life, and most Friday nights they would bring me and my sister to stay at our grandmother's house while they went to one event or another. I looked forward to these sleepovers, for Grandma Rosa (or Rosita, as she was called) was the most amazing woman I'd ever met—always smiling and talking about interesting things, trips, and experiences from throughout her life. My favorite part of these visits was the "tour" of her house, which was like a museum, full of mysterious and delightful objects, each with its own story. As she told me where every object came from, how she got it, and who gave it to her, I felt like I was on a trip to faraway lands, maybe even another planet. I had no idea, though, how much her wisdom would impact my life.

Although I was always excited for Friday night, one in particular stands out in my mind. That night my parents had no plans and I asked if I could sleep at Grandma's anyway. My mother agreed, and—even better—I would be going without my sister. That meant I would have all Grandma's attention, and all her stories, to myself. I would even get to sleep in the same bed!

After setting my backpack down, I followed Grandma for the tour, ready to listen to the story of this porcelain doll, that tea set, or how someone had called her out of nowhere asking if she was interested in seeing a chair from the fifteenth century that once

71

belonged to someone famous. Instead, on that day, Grandma wanted to talk to me about my grandfather, who had passed away before I was born. She started showing me her favorite and most special objects that had been gifted to her by the love of her life. Though each gift was unique, they all had something in common: carved or painted roses on them. This wasn't surprising to me. Grandma's name means "rose," and her house not only smelled like roses, but they appeared on the soaps, linens, tea sets, sofa covers, and paintings. What I was fascinated by, at eight years old, was the idea that someone could be so special in your life, and that the connection between a husband and wife could be so strong even after they were separated by physical death.

Later, as we climbed into her large, very comfy bed, I snuggled close to her, close enough to feel her breathing and the warmth of her body. Really, I wanted to feel protected. I had always been a very light sleeper, wakened by the smallest noise. I also used to hear voices and feel presences in my room, and many nights ended up sleeping next to my mom because I was afraid. It got to the point that my parents took me to therapy to find out what was happening, and the psychologist even came over to see if my house and room was haunted!

Sure enough, I woke in the middle of the night to the sound of voices. I felt some fear, but calmed down when I felt Grandma next to me. I asked her what was going on, and she replied, "Everything is okay, I am just talking to your grandpa. You can go back to sleep." Though I didn't understand what she was talking about, I did feel the presence of someone sitting next to my grandma. This was different from those times in my own bedroom—I felt safe with her next to me and I could feel her laughter and joy in the conversation.

The next day I asked her, "Grandma, were you talking to Grandpa last night, or was I dreaming?"

"Yes," she said, "He visits me almost every night since he was gone. He sits next to me on the bed and we talk and laugh together. You shouldn't be afraid. He was an amazing man and I wish you could have met him."

That became our special secret, and I loved the fact that I knew something about Grandma that no one else did.

My other grandmother, Pepa, also played an enormous role in my life. I grew up in a big family—my mother and father were each one of seven children, so I had lots of cousins, aunts, and uncles. Everything revolved around my two grandmothers; we visited them every weekend, and Sundays belonged to Grandma Pepa. She was the sweetest woman and loved to have tea parties with her granddaughters. I remember her lovely white hair, the smell of her home—like coffee and cake—and the garden that was the perfect place to play. Pepa was Catholic, and I grew up hearing amazing stories of her devotion to Jesus. Years earlier, the night before she was scheduled for eye surgery, she prayed to a wooden statue of Christ in her room, asking for healing. The next day she arrived at the hospital and was told she was completely healed!

But the best story of all was about my dad. One day, when he was nine months old, the nanny took him to sunbathe on the rooftop of their three-floor building. His older brother and sister were running around the house, and my grandpa was about to arrive home for lunch. Suddenly, the nanny came running downstairs, screaming, "It fell, it fell!" Thinking she was talking about a toy, my grandma told her to calm down, go downstairs and just pick it up—they fell off the rooftop all the time. The nanny, shocked and speechless, finally said, "No! it was the baby, the baby fell down!" My grandma went running to the balcony and saw her baby in the main entrance awning of the building, covered with blood. He was rushed to the hospital, and by some miracle, survived. The next day it was on the front page of the newspaper: "Nine-month-old Baby Survives After Falling From the Fourth Floor." My dad's middle name: Jesus!

I was deeply influenced by these amazing grandmothers and their stories as I grew up, dreaming about traveling and conquering the world. And I went on to achieve my dreams—living in Brazil with a great career and a husband. Then one day I received the devastating news that I had cancer in the tear duct of my left eye. It was a very rare, and, as it turned out, symbolic type of cancer.

After that a very special healing journey started, waking me up and showing me how lost and sad I was. The left side of the body is associated with the feminine, and by "crying," my left eye was telling me that I had lost the connection with my feminine wisdom and my intuition. I had also completely forgotten about the childhood voices, the stories, the joy, the curiosity, and—yes—the miracles. And now I had one more miracle to add to the list: I was healed from the cancer.

Shortly after going through the healing process, I was walking to a store close to my house. It was a nice evening, and I remember feeling the gentle breeze on my face. Suddenly, two kids ran past, then looked back at me laughing. I heard this voice inside say, "Run, run like them!" and I thought, "Oh no, they are kids, they can run. I am an adult and it doesn't make sense for me to run like crazy in the middle of the street." I kept walking, and a few meters later a man came running across the street toward me, a knife in his hand. From there, it unfolded like a movie—with him, sweating and nervous as he tried to grab my purse, and me trying to calm him down so I could give it to him without getting stabbed. In the middle of it all, I noticed one of the kids who had passed me a few minutes earlier. He was there watching everything, looking at me in the eyes as if saying, "I tried to help you, but you didn't listen." The guy took my purse and ran away, leaving me unharmed. After that, the voices, gone since childhood, came back, but I didn't pay attention. Life was busy and I had to move on.

Many years later, I was traveling to Austin to meet my amazing

Chapter 7
The Spaces In Between

friends and sisters for a weekend retreat. I flew from Florida to
Houston, then caught a connecting flight to Austin. Never a fan
of airplanes, I had learned to manage my feelings after years of
constant travel, but I remember being tired from a long day at
work as I took my seat by the window. It was dark and rainy, and
before departing the pilot said it was going to be a little bumpy
because of the weather. I opened a book and tried to relax, but the
turbulence, light at first, soon got really bumpy. I started looking
everywhere for the flight attendants—my way of checking to see
if things were okay—but they didn't seem alarmed. Neither did the
other passengers, most of whom were sleeping.

I again tried to relax, but then I saw lightning outside the window.
The airplane started moving like crazy, as if it was made of paper.
People woke up and started making noises, and I could feel the fear
in the air. Then the pilot came on again, telling us we were in the
middle of the storm and he was trying to get out of it. There was no
way to head back, he said, he had to keep on going. Some people
started screaming, others talking loudly, or maybe praying. I was
paralyzed with fear. My neck was hurting, my heart was pounding,
and I had chills. My mind was racing with thoughts that I might
really die that night. Not knowing what else to do, I closed my
eyes, started to meditate, connecting to my breathing, my gut, and
my heart, trying to relax.

Suddenly, in the middle of that crazy storm, I felt a calm like
never before. I felt warm, almost like the sun was rising and entering
through the window, it felt good and peaceful. Then I started hearing
my grandmothers' voices, as clearly as if they were sitting right
there with me, holding my hands. They were telling me to stay calm,
everything would be okay. The more I felt their presence, the calmer
I became. Then they started saying, "Now you have to talk about us,
the grandmothers, to the women, to the girls, to the people of the
world, and bring our message to them." Their names flashed across

my mind as if they were a brand: Rosita & Pepa. I smiled, then I must have fallen asleep because when I opened my eyes again we were about to land in Austin. I was still in shock thinking about all that had happened during that flight, about that message, how clear it was, and how warm it felt. I got off the plane filled with gratitude and excited to tell my friends about the experience.

When I returned home I went into research mode, looking for pictures from my grandmas' lives and asking my parents and relatives for stories. I also started playing with art, symbols, and other things that reminded me of them, thinking about their names and meditating about each of them. One day while in mediation, I was taken back to Grandma Rosita's house, with the roses on her decorations, her furniture, her paintings, and even her clothing. I then clearly saw a beautiful pink rose next to her name.

Then came a memory of being with my sister and cousin in Pepa's garden. We were eating tangerines, talking and laughing, and someone had the idea to plant the tangerine seeds. I remember the smell of the fruit, the feel of the soil on my hands and the wind on my face, and, most importantly, the joy. At that moment I knew that next to Pepa's name I had to have a tangerine and some seeds. Some months later while talking to my cousin about this crazy story—the plane, the names, the memories, and the tangerines—she said, "Do you realize that the name Pepa means "seed" in Spanish?" We were both amazed by how our minds, bodies, senses, and hearts work, together and with our intuition. Everything is connected, we just need to pay attention.

And today, that's what I am doing—listening carefully to the voices, to the signs, to the spaces in between, to what's next, to what's needed. My grandmas keep sending me messages in dreams, in memories, in stories, and through the many wise women that I have connected since creating "Rosita & Pepa" and "Grandma´s March" event. I keep bringing these messages to my day-to-day, to my life, and to others; they connect me back to my soul, to my essence, reminding me every day that I am a miracle, that life is a miracle that happens to all. We just need to listen and believe.

ABOUT THE AUTHOR: Monica Jaramillo is a Shakti Leadership Fellow, Elevate Feminine Leadership Council co-facilitator, and True Purpose® Coach with a passion for people, art, traveling, feminine leadership, and yoga. Born in Medellin, Colombia, she has lived and worked in various countries, which opened her up to different cultures. Monica holds a master's degree in Jungian Psychology and Art Therapy, and for eighteen+ years served as a human resources executive in multinational companies. She is the founder of Rosita & Pepa, a platform to create consciousness around the grandmother archetype, and Grandma's March, an event celebrating feminine wisdom. Monica loves mentoring women in her community and spending time with her nephews, Sebastian and Martin.

Monica Jaramillo
Rosita & Pepa
rositapepa.com
monica@wisexperience.com

Sharing And Receiving
Deep Appreciation And Love

This is a great exercise to help you become aware of the words and actions that spark these feelings within you, and how you can help spark them within others in your life. Have someone you share a business or personal relationship with ask you the following questions. Use the first answer that pops into your mind, as that will be the purest.

Then switch and ask these questions of your partner. Their answers will provide you with the best way to communicate your appreciation or love. This knowledge helps you to adjust your communication for those who are wired differently from you, thus allowing you to connect with people more deeply and share your appreciation and love in ways it can be received.

How You Feel Appreciated

1. Can you remember a time when you felt totally appreciated?
    Be specific. Who were you with? Where were you and what were you doing?

2. How do you know you are totally appreciated?

    a. Is it when you are taken places, brought things, or looked at in that special way?

    b. OR, when you hear a particular tone of voice or special words? What does that tone sound like? What are those words?

    c. OR, is it necessary that you are touched in a certain way or a certain place?

How You Feel Deeply Loved

1. Can you remember a time when you were totally loved? Again, be specific. Who were you with? Where were you and what were you doing?

2. How do you know you are totally loved?

    a. Is it when you are taken places, brought things, or to be looked at in that special way?

    b. OR, when you hear that special tone of voice or particular words?

    c. OR, is it when you are touched in a certain way or a certain place?

---

* This is based on the NLP Deep Love Strategy developed by Bandler and Grinder.

CHAPTER 8

The Path of Most Resistance
Revital Chitayat

I will begin my story where all things start—in the delicious void of infinite possibilities. As I write this, moving forward and backward in time, I am in awe of the many doors that opened every time I agreed to say "yes" to my empathic abilities. Over time, I've learned with quiet certainty that every step I take along my yellow brick road promises to be fulfilling, and purposeful. But there is one little caveat: Trust has been a necessary ingredient in the unfoldment of this extraordinary journey. In order to play this new game defined by new rules and miraculous results, I had to first practice the intricate shades of trust—trusting myself, trusting others, trusting the Universe, and, gradually, learning to trust the validity of my gifts. For this reason, I laughingly call my journey "The Path of Most Resistance"—simply because I resisted it almost every step of the way.

In the past, the notion that I was an "empath" would have been inconceivable. I am a Capricorn, and for much of my life I believed only in what I could experience with my five senses. Any out-of-the-ordinary experience that my rational, left brain could not compute was immediately stored in a "Handle with Care" box, bubbled-wrapped between layers of cynicism, and packed away in a "do not enter" area of my unconscious mind.

To avoid any chance of my repressed spiritual abilities rising to the surface, I became a master of skepticism and doubt. I carefully probed every intuitive thought, diligently researched any Source-inspired decision, and procrastinated. In short, I effectively avoided anything that was remotely classified as "woo woo" (which to me was basically synonymous with "spiritual").

And yet…

Despite my resistance, Empathy chose me, again and again.

I never wanted it.

I did everything I could to avoid it.

But it just kept showing up via spiritual breadcrumbs, little signs along the way; serendipity, synchronicity, knowing things about people or events for which there was no logical explanation.

After years of unbridled sovereignty, my rational mind was beginning to realize that it was fighting a losing battle.

I clearly remember the day it began to shift.

At the time I had already transitioned from successful TV producer to professional life coach. I was certified in several methodologies and always curious to explore new and effective systems leading to a more purposeful life. So when a friend sent me a link to Tim Kelley's *Finding Your True Purpose*, I immediately ordered it. The book had numerous journaling exercises like "talking to your inner skeptic," or exploring the worst-case scenario around your innermost fears. Piece of cake for me. Since I love writing and have been journaling since I was eight, these exercises made sense and I found them enjoyable and useful.

About three-quarters of the way through Kelley mentioned something he called "A Trusted Source." He described having an invaluable connection with these Trusted Sources, one that enabled him to receive high-quality answers to…well, anything, including what I consider to be the ultimate question of all: What is your life's purpose?

I reread the paragraph again, a bit jealous of him for being surrounded by such a caliber of people, friends he deeply trusted, who knew him intimately and took a loving interest in his life. It was something that deeply resonated with me, and although it seemed a bit odd that he would call his best friends "Trusted Sources."

I felt intrigued by this unique partnership that he was describing... until he suggested journaling with my own "Trusted Source."

What?!

I remember the sinking feeling, the all-too-familiar wave of disdain and disgust: "Is he talking about connecting to...his Higher Guidance?!" My brain instantly set off alarm bells of "Resist! Resist! Resist!"

How could this guy—rational, intelligent, and obviously "normal"—buy into this stuff?

My inner Capricorn was outraged, reminding me that I only believe in "real things" and "the real world." So I closed the book, ready to bubble wrap and pack it away as I had done to so many other "outside the logic box" things over the years. Only this time, I couldn't. For the first time in my life, my reliable "trust your five senses only" detector had turned itself off.

A few days later, after a morning of Mommy-Taxi duties, I was sitting at a small coffee shop waiting for the heavy traffic to subside. I had found the perfect table beneath a willow tree and was enjoying a strong cappuccino and a decadent almond croissant. Since I journal almost daily, it seemed natural to use this perfect setting, take out my new journal, and write.

But on that particular morning, it felt like my writing was guided by something other than my rational mind. The words appeared faster than I could write, as I described a journey toward a sunlit mountain, a mystical cave, and a translucent pool of exquisite beauty. Through the words, I saw myself looking into the water, discovering the image of a beautiful woman dressed in green. And there she was: My Trusted Source.

The pen moved swiftly across the page, almost against my will and, all the while I kept telling myself that "This is ridiculous!" and "I'm obviously making this up." But I couldn't stop writing. Despite my well-rehearsed resistance, I received an extraordinary glimpse of a connection that would transform my entire belief system, define my purpose, and deeply enrich my life.

Looking back, my ability to sense or read others had always been there. From childhood, my loved ones teasingly referred to my empathic awareness of the energy in a room as being a "bleeding heart." I was contemptuous of my overwhelming ability to see, hear, and feel others on intimate levels, critically defining it as being a "people-pleaser."

As I backtracked along my path of most resistance, things began to make sense. I seemed to know, with a sudden expansion in my heart, the core of a person's emotional blocks. I could easily recognize repeated patterns of behavior, connecting seemingly unrelated dots to create a meaningful picture. A masterpiece. I could always see the grander vision of people and situations with a sense of wonder at the image of who they could become.

But over time, these gifts became a burden for me. I was increasingly aware of my empathic abilities and was feeling exhausted from the sense that I was somehow responsible for others. I suddenly realized that once upon a time, in order to keep this ability in check, I had made an unconscious choice to tone it all down. I chose a colorful career as a TV and commercial producer, which enabled me to make the most of my "picture-seeing" abilities while remaining safely behind the scenes.

Fast forward a few decades and there I was, sitting beneath the willow tree, watching words that were not mine appear on the page: *Procrastination time is over.* I wrote words that were seemingly being dictated to me. *You will eventually release the doubt which has been a comfort to you. No, there is nothing to forgive. This was your path to explore, this was what you are here to release. Would you expect a fish to ask forgiveness for swimming? Be good to yourself.*

I kept writing, hearing, feeling the words, too stunned to stop. *You are a messenger.* I wrote with alarm bells ringing in my head. *You will lead others; people will follow you because of who you are and what you stand for.*

At this point, I laughed out loud.

A messenger?! Lead others? Are you kidding me? I had just recently been certified as a coach and was still struggling to fill my clinic. And I was a full-time mom, a role I took very seriously. So the only people "following" me at that time were my three beloved babies.

I remember the instant relief, realizing that this was a wacky trick of my unconscious mind.

Seriously. Me? A leader? Not.

Yet I felt compelled to continue writing the words I heard in my imagination.

You are right. You are a mother. And mothers lead quietly. With love. They do not need the limelight, for they are the light. You will lead quietly, like you always do.

I felt nauseous. It was as if ten thousand butterflies had suddenly flown straight up from the pit of my stomach. *You are the gentle light of motherly love. You heal the wings of those who want to fly. Like guiding a child on his first bike ride—not too much so he loses faith in himself, not too little so he falls. You have the inherent sense to do this just right.*

It went on and on, this voice that I felt and heard.

I received clear instructions on what to do—from cleaning the clutter on my desk to starting a meditation practice (and just to be clear: at the time, the very word "meditation" made me wince in disgust). As I wrote, my carefully paved path of resistance began to crack.

I had been so deeply engrossed in my writing that I was shocked when the waitress came over to ask me if I was ready to order lunch.

"You looked so intense," she said with a smile, "that none of us wanted to disturb you. Are you writing a book?"

"Not yet," I answered and rushed back to the comfort of a busy, no-time-to-think day.

But every once in a while I'd stop and ask myself: What just happened? And more importantly—what if it happens again?

I put away my journal and didn't dare to touch it for weeks.

Still, I found myself clearing my desk, checking out different approaches to meditation, and trying to research this inexplicable voice or presence which I could not understand in any rational way.

The only thing I knew beyond a doubt was that there was no possible way I could have invented any of the things I wrote. Light… Love…Leadership…Wing healing…every time I thought about them, I literally felt sick (a tell-tale sign of intuitive content for us resistant messengers.) These were one-hundred-percent bubble-wrappable words straight from the danger zone which I had been so careful to avoid.

Many weeks later, I finally opened the journal again.

Hesitantly at first, and then with a growing sense of confidence, I asked questions, endless questions about…everything.

And I received profound answers—creative, brilliant, inspiring ideas that I started to share with a few close friends who I knew were "safe."

The more I dared to show up, the clearer the connection with this "voice" became, so I wrote journals upon journals of exploration.

At some point I stopped trying to understand how it works, this very loving connection, and chose to simply listen. I released the many little "Truth Tests" I'd created and slowly taught myself how to trust. I got lost and found. I released layers of fear and doubt. I healed childhood wounds and received inspired guidance on how to do the same with others. I chose a new, less taken road. And with every new experience, I learned to release my debilitating habit of playing hide and seek with myself, my higher guidance, and my life's purpose.

I stopped running away, announcing that "This can't be real," "I sound crazy"; and "It's just not who I am" and instead, chose to live my calling and become an ever-expanding version of myself. I became the leader that once upon a time, beneath a willowy willow, I was told I would be.

When we doubt trust, we move through life along this path of most resistance, effort, and pain. Life is unsafe and we must be prepared for the worst—which is always lurking right around the corner.

When we begin to doubt Doubt, we are willing to question our thoughts' conclusions and painful "Life Truths" we created. And this allows for the shift to begin. It is the essential crack necessary to question everything we know and think we know, in order to open the possibility to experience something new.

When we trust Trust, we learn to trust ourselves, our instincts, feelings, empathic gifts and intuitive guidance. Our life journey shifts from a path driven by fear…to an ongoing adventure guided by freedom.

This is a choice I make, over and over again with ever-expanding ripples of impact on the world around me. It has guided me towards the enlightened partnerships I've formed, the successful projects I've created, the inspired content I teach. And yes, every once in a while I still resist, when the leap of faith feels too high or when the need for exposure feels too great or too bright.

Yet, there always comes a point at which I stop, breathe, release the fear, and say "I do," to this extraordinary gift.

For me, this is the ultimate reminder of our human ability to choose, commit, heal, create, explore, rise to the occasion, fall and rise again and again, learn a new game with new rules that offer the ultimate freedom to become the greatest version of what we might be.

And in the process, to create a meaningful life worth living.

ABOUT THE AUTHOR: Revital Chitayat is a Professional Lifechanger. She has worked internationally with hundreds of people, teaching them to transform their Inner Dialogue, connect with their Higher Guidance, and manifest their passions and purpose. She is a speaker, intuitive guide, and mentor, certified in a variety of methodologies. Following a successful career as a TV and commercial producer, she decided to embark on a "Path of Most Resistance" to discover her calling, guiding reluctant messengers to manifest their full potential, and enabling them to expand their influence in the world. She resides in Israel, happily married and mother to three extraordinary human beings.

Revital Chitayat
revitalcoach@gmail.com
Cell: ++972-52-8877877
Facebook: facebook.com/revitalcoach

EMPATH TOOL
by Jade Rehder

ASK Yourself

Do you find yourself seeking answers about your life from external sources, only to feel more confused than ever? Do you know that you have the amazing ability to get these answers for yourself by communicating with your subconscious / body/mind? Well, you do! A friend of mine recently experienced this practice while sitting in a coffee shop. By simply asking herself yes or no questions, she was able to access her inner knowing for the next steps in creating her dream business. "I have been asking everyone else what they thought about what I was doing," she exclaimed excitedly. "Now I have the power to ask myself!" Using the ASK Yourself practice, you can confirm what you have felt is the right action for you, rather than relying on other, often conflicting voices that may lead to overwhelm or confusion.

Determining Your Yes and No Directions

- Before you begin, make sure there is plenty of room around you.

- Stand up, with your feet close together and your knees slightly bent.

- Call in your high self—"In the name of the Light I call in my High Self" (this allows only the aspects of the high self that are of the Light to be influencing).

- Relax and connect to your body.

- Now, out loud, ASK your body/mind this question: "Subconscious / body/mind, show me an undeniable sway of my body that represents the answer YES."

- Your body will move in whatever direction it wants and that is your YES direction. (It may move backward, forward, left, right, or at an angle—whichever way it goes is right for you.)

- Thank your subconscious / body/mind for answering you.

- Next, ASK this question: "Subconscious / body/mind, show me an undeniable sway of my body that represents the answer NO."

- The direction your body moves is your NO direction.

- Thank your subconscious / body/mind connected with your pure high consciousness for answering you.

- Now, ASK Yourself questions with yes or no answers.

When you are good at the practice you can ask the questions silently. Make sure you check your yes and no directions as you make changes because your directions may shift.

To take this practice further, you can use it while shopping; for example, "Will I wear this pair of shoes enough to justify buying them?" or "What does my body want to eat to provide the needed nutrients and nutrition for me to be fit and feel well? Broccoli or chocolate?" (To test food, hold it between your heart and throat to access the thymus gland.) You get the idea!

CHAPTER 9

Visits With God
Millie America

The first time I met God, I was in the hospital. I had been rushed there after waking up in a park at midnight with a massive knot on the back of my head and another on my forehead. But that was the least of it. I also thought I was nineteen years old, when in fact I was thirty-three, with six children and a different husband. Just like that, fourteen years had disappeared from my memory.

Needless to say, my life was completely turned upside down and, that first night, I was coming undone. The thought of going home to a house I didn't recognize and a family I couldn't remember was terrifying. All night I cried in pain and fear; the next morning the neurologist performed a spinal tap, a frightening procedure that left spinal fluid leaking from my back and me unable to think straight. When midnight rolled around again, a nurse came in to check my vitals. She was lovely and bodacious, with a thick Jamaican accent. She pulled up a chair from against the wall, sat near my bed, and asked what happened to me. I couldn't remember.

Her name tag read Cinthya, and I commented that I had never seen the name spelled with a "y" at the end. She smiled, then, gently taking my hand, Cinthya asked several questions. Though I couldn't answer most of them, I sobbed to this stranger as if I had known her for years.

"Why do you think this happened to you? Why would you lose fourteen years of your life?" she asked.

"I don't know. I only know that I don't want to go home to those strangers." I wiped the flood of tears.

"You know that everything has a divine purpose. I can bet that years from now you will see this moment as a pivotal wake-up call of sorts." She smelled like roses as she came closer to me.

"I can't imagine what this is teaching me," I said, suddenly drowsy. The last thing I remember was closing my eyes.

Hours later, when another nurse came in to check my vitals, I asked her to please tell Cinthya to come by before her shift was over. The nurse told me there was no one on the floor by that name. I described the woman who had been so kind to me, but she insisted that there were only two nurses on the wing; plus, she had been working in the hospital for eight years and had never met such a person. She then asked if maybe I had dreamed it.

I pointed to the chair next to my bed and said, "She pulled that chair there and we spoke for a long time. She had a name tag and was dressed in white."

There are times I have questioned my sanity and imagination. Was Cinthya real? Was she an angel? But what IS real? Over the next decade I would begin unraveling those questions, and what I realized is that it's all about perception. If I experienced something in my life then it's real to me. The more I dove into my spiritual practice, the more real it became.

During those ten years Cinthya began showing up in my meditations. She let me know that she was my virtual picture of God. Since that night in the hospital I'd learned that her unusual name means "light or to uncover" and, indeed, our visits to the spiritual realm always revealed and illuminated the things I need to learn. I also began to see God everywhere, whether I was awake or asleep. Sometimes He was dressed as regular folks with messages; other times She appeared as Keanu Reeves or Richard Gere in my dreams. God's presence had taught me to be present and mindful, and before I knew it I was taking notice of every single conversation with every person, and often feeling deep connections to these everyday sages. Yet, when I went into meditation, She continued to show up as the beautiful woman with the lilting accent I had fallen in love with.

I never know how or when God will visit me. One of Her strongest messages came when I was in the middle of a nasty separation. My relationship had deteriorated and I wanted guidance as to what I could do to heal myself. While in meditation, I found myself visiting God in Her little "casita" by the water. This was not surprising, as that's always the safest and most loving place for me to meet Her. From the outside, the "casita" doesn't look like much more than a shack, but once I step in, it has the warmth of love. And it always smells like my grandmother's bread pudding.

On this particular day God was working outside. She handed me a basket and told me we would be picking bananas. I didn't want to pick bananas. I was lucky to have a connection to the Divine and I wanted answers about my relationship. Nevertheless, I found myself following God around as She shared tidbits about the many species of bananas on the earth. Finally, She took the basket from me and set it down on the sand. She then took a green banana and opened it up so I could eat it.

"I don't like green bananas."

"That's right. You like your bananas bruised, like your men."

After a moment I took the banana from Her outstretched hand and, from the first bite, felt the truth of Her words.

This is the sort of thing that sticks out when God speaks to me. I make it a point of paying attention to every word and gesture. Nothing goes unnoticed.

My interactions with the Divine are beautiful now, but I didn't always experience them that way. Certainly, being visited by passed-on ancestors as a child wasn't easy. As early as three or four, they started coming to me, wanting to talk. The first to show up was my paternal grandmother, who had died way before I was conceived.

At the time my mother and I lived in a small house in Puerto Rico. In my bedroom Mom had placed a stationary bike for her to exercise. One night I was woken up by the sound of someone riding the bike. I sat up on my bed and saw an older woman I didn't recognize peddling away. When she saw me staring she got off the bike and came close to the bed. After asking me not to be afraid (I wasn't, just curious and a little confused) she said she was my grandmother and that she was always watching me. She also told me I had gotten my middle name, America, from her. Finally, she told me that I would be visited by many other ancestors because I had the gift of communication.

Weeks later I told my mother after she heard me talking alone in my room. She asked me to describe the woman I had seen, then found a photo of my grandmother that was exactly how she had appeared to me. My mother didn't know what to do with me and these conversations. They scared her. I would know things before they happened. She took me to therapists, spiritualists, and finally a doctor. At the age of six I had come to believe that these "gifts," as my grandmother called them, were anything but. In fact, they caused such severe anxiety for me and my mother that I made it a point to stop listening and seeing.

Still, the anxiety continued as I was growing up, for although I refused to entertain the spiritual realm I could feel them around me. I just couldn't label what I was feeling. Because of this, I didn't feel normal. I didn't feel like I fit anywhere. I felt a sense of disconnection from my family and friends. I didn't want to be distracted by these "gifts." But guess what happens when you resist the truth of who you are? The lessons become even harder. They keep showing up until you address the underlying issue. My issue was avoiding the intuitive messages because I didn't want to be labeled as "crazy" or "witchy."

Yet I could always feel God; I could feel Him/Her with me.

And, that night in the hospital all those years later, God showed me that my gifts had never gone away. I just had to be moved out of the way so I could recognize that I was always being held in grace.

These days I embrace the visions, the knowing, the visitations, and everything else that I used to avoid. I am healthier because I have stepped into my gifts. I am also able to help others because of those "knowings."

On January 15, 2014, eleven years after the amnesia, I ended up in the hospital again, this time with chest pains that the doctors thought first to be a heart attack, then a stroke. As they worked to save me I slipped away, into that in-between place that millions have experienced during NDEs (near-death experiences). If you have ever watched "The Matrix," it was like that white room that's not of the fake world they're living in, but nor is it the reality. It was so bright that I couldn't tell the floor from the walls or the ceiling. I also, for the first time in my life, felt this indescribable sense of peace, along with an unconditional love that took every phobia and fear I'd ever had.

While there I heard voices of loved ones in the distance. I felt the presence of God (I knew that frequency well!) I also saw my father, who had not been present in my life and passed when I was in my late twenties. Suddenly, my *papito* was there, pulling me into a hug.

"*Mija*, it's so good to see you. I am so proud of you," he said as he held me.

"Papi, I cannot believe I am here with you." I held onto his warm hands.

"Millie, you have to go back."

"Nah, I'm good. This is a wonderful place. I want to be with you and Mami."

"Mija, they had to take you out of the way to give you an upgrade. It's not your time."

"Papi, I don't know who 'they' are but I can assure you that I am exactly where I need to be."

Abruptly, I was pushed back into my physical body. My fiancé was by my side, holding my hands. I learned that what the doctors thought was a heart attack or stroke was actually a massive panic attack. Also, what had felt like hours in that white room was only a few minutes in our earthly dimension. Now I had returned with a deep, unsettling awareness of everything around me. I was given water and I felt heightened sensations as it traveled down my throat. And when my fiancé kissed me, I felt like it was the first kiss ever.

As days turned into weeks, I was slower than my previous self. I could hear the earth stretching under the snow. I could hear and taste colors. I was overwhelmed with voices from the esoteric world. I slowed down a lot that winter. I allowed for messages. I was not the same person and those around me feared that I would check out for good. The thoughts were very present during those days. I wanted to feel what I had experienced in that realm. I wanted to have no more human suffering.

Spirit has a magnificent way of teaching us about our purpose. We all have contracts of things to do and experience that we created before our incarnations, but that doesn't mean they are all going to be fun. In fact, they are often painful and exhausting. Truly, this human experience is not for sissies! That NDE taught me that fear is an illusion, and that the "gifts" from childhood were beautiful. I was also no longer able to avoid the visions.

God continues to visit me often, or maybe it is I who visits Her. Either way, we get a lot of screen time in my meditations. She continues to show me things before they happen. She makes sure I pay close attention to signs. And this is how I now experience life, as a scavenger hunt, waiting for beautiful signs from the other dimension.

A few months ago, I finally stepped into giving one-on-one private sessions to clients. At first it was scary. My self-worth/ego kept telling me that I shouldn't do any sessions. "Who are you, Millie? What messages do you think you can give anyone?"

Amazing what happens when we shut the ego and move through our higher purpose! Folks get lovely messages from their loved ones and there is a healing available to them. My life would have been so much easier if I hadn't resisted my divine gifts as a child, or if I had listened to Cinthya twenty years ago. But, oh, the lessons I have learned along the way have been invaluable.

And my message to you? DO NOT suppress who you are! You are an empath and that is a massive superpower. Love yourself enough to recognize and embrace it!

ABOUT THE AUTHOR: Millie America is a story-tender, writer, metaphysical facilitator, authenticity mentor, intuitive empath, and multidimensional healer, helping others navigate the muck of daily life to reach their own inner beauty and strength. Just like the lotus flower, we all have the willingness and determination to be the best version of ourselves while birthing in the darkest of moments. Sometimes we need a little help, and Millie is a loving cheerleader, helping us connect with our ancestors and one another so we recognize that we are never alone on this journey.

Millie America
sacredjourneyinward.com
sacredjourneyinward@gmail.com
828-707-8897

Filling Up with Light, Joy, and Happiness

Picture being in a special spot where you have had an intense experience of Light, Joy, and Happiness. Go deep into the details, allowing yourself to create the movie of this place in your mind's eye. If none come to mind, it's all good. Use the power of your imagination to pretend one into creation!

Now, whether you are tapping into a vivid past experience or creating a new special spot, answer these questions and fill up with light, joy, and happiness!

- What are you seeing in your mind's eye? Notice all the details—images, sounds, feelings, and thoughts.

- Bring the images into sharp focus.

- Brighten the colors.

- Take a moment and listen to what you hear in your special spot.

- Turn up the sounds that increase your feelings of happiness, joy, and light.

- What encouraging words are you saying to yourself? Yes, hear your inner cheerleader!

- Increase the volume on your positive soundtrack!

- What do you notice about the feeling(s) these images and

sounds are creating inside you?

- Tap into these juicy feelings and increase them like waves. Allow them to wash over you. Be with this for a couple of minutes.

- Do you sense a new stream of Light flowing into your energy field and body? It may have a color, tone, feeling, or you may just know it's with you.

- Ask to preserve this flow of energy in your field multidimensionally, filling yourself up with light, joy, and happiness!

CHAPTER 10

Miracles of Trust
Kara Valentine

Growing up, I always had a guttural reaction to witnessing people suffer. I was the kid who would cry at commercials, despair after watching the news, and crumble when people close to me were in pain. A movie where a mom or child passed away unexpectedly—forget about it! I would be a mess for days.

It was quite a paradox because I had a difficult time accessing and feeling my own feelings. As a survivor of childhood sexual abuse, I did everything in my power to avoid being alone and pretend that everything was okay. However, when there was pain to feel for others, I would let it loose. I remember running on a treadmill at the neighborhood gym and watching the news coverage of the Haiti earthquake. What started as tears welling up in my eyes ended with me bent over my treadmill sobbing. I'll never forget the look in the woman's eyes as she ran with her lifeless child in her arms, screaming for someone to help her. I looked around at my fellow exercisers, whose workouts continued uninterrupted, and thought, *How were they all okay witnessing this level of devastation?*

In my early adult life, my sister and I read *The Secret Life of Bees*. There is a character named May, who suffers from depression and deeply feels the suffering of humanity. Her sisters recommend that she build a "wailing wall" that she can visit when she is overwhelmed by tragic news. May starts a ritual in which she writes down what is causing her despair in the hopes that it would dissipate; instead, it all becomes too much for her and she ends her life. I remember relating to May in many ways (my sister actually recommended that I build my own wailing wall); I also remember how she was portrayed as not being "okay" and that her sensitivity was a problem. I could really relate to that as well.

In addition to my sensitivity to suffering, I also hated witnessing disparity. This showed up in all kinds of ways, from counting Christmas presents under the tree to be sure my siblings and I all received the same to being a stickler for rules on the playground at recess. If I was involved, you bet things were going to be fair. What showed up as an annoying trait in its earliest expression has turned into my drive to create and engage in a world that is equitable, connected, and loving.

After traveling the world and seeing extreme poverty up close, my best friends and I had spent years trying to figure out how we could run a business that really made a difference. Seeing women and children begging in the streets created a deeper inner conflict. It felt wrong to give them money, like perpetuating an inhumane and unsustainable way of living, and yet not giving it to them felt like turning a blind eye.

In 2011, we started Threads Worldwide, a social enterprise committed to bringing connection and empowerment to women around the world. We do this by creating partnerships between women artisans in developing countries and women here in the US, who create a marketplace for these beautiful handmade products.

Looking back, it feels like a miracle that we trusted ourselves to take this leap. On paper, we had *no* business starting the business that we did, especially given what was happening in my life at the time.

I had recently returned home from a three-month stay at the hospital with my teeny tiny infant, Bryn, who came into the world ten weeks before her due date and weighing a whopping two pounds. There had been no indicators during the pregnancy that an infection was brewing in my amniotic fluid, but thankfully my body saw the danger and pushed Baby Bryn into this world and the care of neonatal specialists.

Now here I was, the mother of a baby that was slightly longer than a dollar bill and looked more like a newborn chicken than a child. Bryn spent the first part of her life in a heated incubator, not being able to be held or comforted. Tubes were connected to the vast majority of her body. I felt mostly numb and concentrated on doing whatever people around me told me to do. I believed she would live or die based on her doctors' efforts.

My Aunt Jane called to check in on Bryn (and me) on a day when I was feeling like all hope was lost. In fact, we had just spoken with the doctors, who gently told us to prepare ourselves for the worst—as if parents could ever prepare themselves for such a thing. Jane had been on a spiritual quest since she was a child. She had once fallen out of a tree only to be caught and laid on the ground by an unknown force. While her "day job" is as an IT professional at a prestigious university, her life's passion is exploring and understanding consciousness. With my permission, Jane and her friends had been gathering to send light and love to our sweet baby.

"I have a message for you about Bryn," she said. "Would you like to hear it?"

I was open to anything at this point and told her I would. "Three things," she said. "Bryn gets scared when you leave. Talk to her about where you are going and when you will be back. Reassure her that you will always be there for her and that she won't have to do this alone. She also needs a vision of the future that is filled with love, hope, and fun. Talk to her about what she has to look forward to if she stays. Let her know that it won't be just living in a hospital hooked up to tubes and feeling separated from her family. Lastly, she needs help getting focused. She needs to know what to heal. From her side, she's trying to do everything at once. Work with the doctors to figure out what is most critical, and then ask her to concentrate on healing that part first."

I don't remember questioning whether this would work, or whether I believed or disbelieved. All I remember is the feeling of relief that I now had something tangible that might make a difference for our girl. From that day on, I spent much of my time whispering in Bryn's ear, telling her all that she had to look forward to by staying and being part of our family. "You will be a flower girl in your Aunt Melissa's wedding this summer. You have a big sister named Avery that you will get to play with and be best friends with forever. You have a mom and dad who will love you with everything they have," and so on and so forth. I checked in with the doctors, asking, "What's the most critical thing right now?" When they told me, "Her kidneys," I relayed this to Bryn. "It's your kidneys, baby girl. Send all of your love and light to your kidneys. You can do this."

The next day there was incredible news: her kidneys were dramatically improved! The doctors were incredulous. I was invigorated. At last, I saw a new future for our Bryn. She would heal and we would take her home. Next up, her lungs. "It's your lungs now, baby. It's your lungs. Heal those lungs. You can do this. I know you can." Two weeks later, she breathed on her own. I continued talking to my tiny daughter every day for the next eighty days until she was well enough to come home. Over the course of those eighty days, she healed her kidneys, her lungs, and her heart; she healed every infection, resolved every barrier to healthy eating, and miraculously doubled her body weight.

Bryn wasn't the only miracle we brought home that day. I came home a different mother. A mother who is deeply in tune with the connection between herself and her child. A mother who knows that she is powerful beyond comprehension. A mother who not only nurtures, soothes, and cheerleads, but who sees what's possible and empowers her children to engage with that world of possibility.

Bryn was now home, but still on oxygen, and I spent my

days meeting with occupational therapists, physical therapists, nutritionists, and other professionals who were helping address her myriad health needs. I also had a rambunctious two-year-old, who was very interested in having her mommy's attention. On top of that, I was working two jobs from home. I wasn't sleeping a whole lot, nor did I feel like I had a single iota left to give.

Enter my best friend, Angela, with her brilliant business idea: "We should import products from women in developing countries and sell through a direct sales channel in the US, creating global connection and empowerment." I looked at her in disbelief. Not only was this terrible timing, but it didn't even make any sense, given our lack of experience in this field.

"Let me get this straight," I said. "We have no international development experience, no retail experience, no direct sales experience, and you want to do *what* exactly?"

"I know it doesn't make sense and I know it's what we are supposed to do," she said with complete conviction.

It was at that moment my intuition kicked in. I thought about how close I had come to losing Bryn and knew that if she had been born in any of the countries we had visited she would have died at birth. I also knew that if I hadn't trusted Jane's message from beyond and engaged with my healing abilities, she wouldn't be by my side today. Now I had the opportunity to pour my heart and soul into a business that would create opportunities for women across the globe to meet the needs of their children. Once I made that realization, I knew this was what I was meant to do.

I have spent the last ten years working to get more comfortable with my inherent empathic gifts. I let my ability to feel others' pain guide me in my decision-making. I started to understand the power of getting quiet and allowing guidance to arrive. I stopped trying to live by the status quo and started challenging it. I got really curious about how I could utilize my gifts and talents to create a movement to change the way the world operates. This was not always smooth sailing, and it's taken years for me to really believe that I have the power to change the way the game is played. There were many meetings when I didn't speak up for the fear of being judged for my "creative" thinking, many years in which I engaged in numbing behaviors to quiet the voice in my gut and the knowing in my heart.

One night, I awoke in the middle of the night with a download of epic proportions: "I am alive at this moment to emerge a new paradigm of business and leadership that can transform the world." I realized that all global systemic suffering—war, exploitation, poverty, trafficking, et cetera—would cease if we shifted one damaging fundamental belief system: one that tells us there is such a thing as an "other" and that life is a win-lose proposition.

I started to think about how things work in nature (i.e. ecosystems) and for the first time started getting interested in science (who knew THAT was possible). I learned about the difference between parasitic relationships—in which one organism (the parasite) gains while the other (the host) suffers—and mutualistic relationships, in which both partners benefit. I realized that most of our world works within a parasitic framework—no wonder I had such a hard time witnessing pain and suffering. I wasn't broken, I was simply paying attention.

What I considered to be weaknesses for much of my life— my sensitivities, big feelings, and reactions—are actually part of my superpower. As women, we are inherently collaborative, compassionate, intuitive, and empathetic. We lead with our hearts and envision ourselves as part of the whole. These values—which I believe will save the world—have been undermined and devalued over the course of history, with women across the globe being told that they have no place in business, in politics, or in any position of power.

I know that I am here to be a disruptor of systems that hold humanity down and help build those that elevate it. Through our Threads Movement, my partners and I have created an environment that calls forth each of our unique gifts and talents, knowing that tapping into them makes individuals feel more alive, more fulfilled, and more able to contribute in the way they are meant to. We also celebrate our differences and understand that our collective power is what will change lives. We understand the interconnectedness of all things. We trust ourselves and we trust one another. This is what it means to channel and transmute the pain we feel on behalf of the world. This is what it means to be an empath.

ABOUT THE AUTHOR: Kara Valentine is a social impact entrepreneur, an innovative thought leader, a passionate humanitarian, and the mother of two brave, beautiful daughters. Kara is a Founder and Chief Community Officer of Threads Worldwide, a social enterprise that provides life-changing work with women around the world through the fair trade of artisan jewelry. Kara is pioneering a revolutionary ideology called The Elevation Ecosystem in an effort to replace our current paradigm of leadership with one that is rooted in connection, inclusion, and collective elevation. Kara holds a B.A. from Tufts University and an M.A. in Counseling Psychology from the University of Colorado at Denver.

Kara Valentine
Threads Worldwide
threadsworldwide.com
kara@threadsworldwide.com

Knobs and Dimmers

Have you been in a situation that sent you into sensory overload? It could have been a crowded place like the line for a sporting event, or the buzz of emotions and talking at a business networking event. No matter what is happening outside, you have the power to reduce the amount, and volume of, the feelings, sensations, and experiences you are taking in.

At other times, such as a trip to the ocean, you may want to expand your sensory intake to fully enjoy the feeling of the sun on your face, the sound of the waves, the breeze in your hair, and the smell of the tropical flowers.

Turn it Down (or Up!)

This is a quick, easy, and fun practice to adjust the level of your sensory experience using imaginary knobs and dimmer switches.

- First, imagine that you have two sets of adjusters—internal and external.

- The internal knobs and dimmers regulate what you are experiencing due to energy, feelings, and emotions created inside you. I find it's best to keep my internal knobs set to the middle—this way I can be aware of and feel my feelings of all kinds, which allows me to listen to my inner knowing more clearly. In the middle position, I can fully experience the pleasure of life with room to reduce it when needed or raise it when I want to really feel something good.

- The external knobs and dimmers allow you to adjust the amount of energy, emotion, sensation, thoughts, sounds, light, and more coming into your experience from outside sources in any given moment or situation.

- This is very simple. Just close your eyes and imagine the knob or dimmer for a particular feeling or external stimulus. See or pretend your hand is turning whatever is bothering you down or dimming it. This tool is as powerful as your imagination. Remember, you can turn the good stuff up too!

- This tool is great when you have no control of the outer world (i.e., the noise and lights in a casino on the Las Vegas strip), or when in situations that are overwhelming. Yet it is no bypass to your inner emotions as they will come to the surface at some time. It is beneficial to turn things down, then, when you have the time and space, be present with the energy. Feel the feels and they will flow through.

EMPATH TOOL
by Jade Rehder

Quiet Time Drive

Where does your mind go when you are quiet with yourself? Your "to-do" list? Does your internal voice start listing what you don't like, want to be, or have happen in your life? Have you been looking for a way to quiet your mind so you can meditate more easily?

The following practice is a wonderful way to expand your awareness and allow more opportunities for creativity.

- Set your phone on silent before you get into the vehicle.

- Turn the radio off and start driving.

- Now it's just you, your thoughts, and the silence.

- Pay attention to your driving.

- How do you feel?

- What do you notice around you?

- What thoughts are coming up?

- Is it comfortable to be alone with yourself?

- Start with a short drive (10 to 15 minutes). To or from work is a great option if your commute is quick.

- The goal is to make the conscious choice between adding distraction and being in silence.

Take this practice to the next level by bringing a notebook or journal with you. When you reach your destination, write what came to mind, both negative and positive, and what you learned during the drive. If you have done a dive into lower vibration, you might try one of the other practices in this book, such as WHAT IF...Spiral Up or Unplug, (See pages 47 and 199) to shift the energy.

CHAPTER 11

Life in Color
Cathy Balken

*I have a secret. I see people in color. At first, it was just that.
Then I realized that I could feel what they were feeling and
hear what they were thinking, across boundaries, languages,
time, and space. Where did this come from? How did this
happen?*

Seventeen years ago, I died. I remember parts of that day. The
sun was bouncing across the hood of my car, dancing on my
windshield with the leafy shadows from the elms above. I was
weaving through the streets in my mom's green, full-sized sedan,
and going way too fast. I glanced at the clock—3:20. I had to make
a choice: deliver these phones to a demanding client or pick my
son up from summer camp. I chose wrong. Back and forth I went,
unable to find the manufacturing plant. GPS never works well in
the mountains and my internal GPS was broken as well.

I was still driving around, and growing more frustrated by the
minute, when my client called.

"Where are you?" he demanded, "I need those phones."

"I am on my way. I should be there at four."

"Well, where *exactly* are you?"

He seemed to know that I was lost.

I was so caught up in getting to him that I didn't see the dually
truck barreling towards the intersection. I am told that the driver
T-boned my car, driving it into a ditch, and then ran me over. The
irony—he was an ER nurse who had worked all night and was
hurrying to get home. He called MAMA (the hospital helicopter),
then 911. When the medics arrived, they closed the highway and

used the jaws of life to cut me out of the crumpled sedan.

"We can't get a pulse," one of them told MAMA. "We are trying to revive her now."

In the meantime, I was flying above the accident. I could see myself lying on the ground, covered in glass and blood. I was wearing my favorite pants—black with cargo pockets. My cell phone rang. A policeman answered it sternly.

"Uh, is Cathy there?" It was my client.

"She has been involved in a serious car accident. Who is this?"

There was stunned silence on the other end, followed by, "I am so sorry. Is she okay? Oh, this is my fault."

"Are you next of kin?"

"Please, just tell me she'll be okay."

"Turn on the news," the policeman answered, then hung up. Around me, the world was whirring; my lifeless shell was hoisted into a helicopter. The scenes were ebbing and flowing in my mind, flashing in and out. Here and there. But where is there?

This next part is fuzzy. I was kneeling before God. He told me I had to go back. I did not have a choice. There were still things I needed to do, but I would be given a gift. I immediately dismissed this part. I didn't care about what I needed to do, or this "gift" He was talking about. All I cared about was living. I couldn't leave my family, my husband, my kids, my parents. I can't tell you where I was, just what happened next. I was flying again, this time above my ICU hospital bed. My leg was in traction. Tumbling down, I was returned to my body. But I had lost something—what had I lost? I tried to open my eyes and look around; I was in a tunnel, and it was so dark. I couldn't see but I could hear.

"Cathy?" My husband Joe was at my side. "Wake up!"

The doctor urged him to keep trying. "She's been in a coma; it's going to take her a while to come to."

Joe saw me stir and said, "You've been in a car accident."

Fear gripped me. "The kids? Are the kids okay? Were they with me?"

To my great relief, he replied, "No, you were alone."

The truck, I thought. "Was anyone else hurt?"

He took my hand and quickly reassured me, "No, he is fine."

I remember thinking, *Thank God,* then I drifted back into the darkness.

***

THE DAY OF: My son Brendan said he was following Joe as he rushed through the hospital corridors. No one had come to pick him up from summer camp; now he had overheard the news that I had no pulse. Thinking he would never see me again, he felt lightheaded and about to pass out. Suddenly he felt hands go under his arms, lift him up, and carry him as he walked; it was like he was floating. Looking back, he felt he was carried by angels at the time he needed them most.

DAY 4: When my eyes opened I was alone in the room and my leg was held up by pins. I couldn't feel it because they had me doped up on pain meds, but when I tried to lean up I saw stars, the pain in my hip was so great. If I had to compare natural childbirth to this pain (a crushed pelvis), I would say it was not even close. I had no idea that, though overpowering, this pain would eventually become my friend. The doctor flew into the room, his white tailcoat trying to keep up with him. He was checking a tube running into my lungs. I had tubes running in and out of my entire body. As he worked I saw, all around him, an indigo outline. *What the—?* Nurses streamed in—pink, light blue, grey—each one a different color. The doctor yanked the tube from my lungs and practically ran from the room. I took my first breath in days. They increased my pain meds and I drifted back off to sleep.

DAY 7: Now in a wheelchair, I had been taken by the nurses to a psychiatrist's office in another part of the hospital.

"Are you experiencing any strange thoughts? You have a mild

traumatic brain injury from your accident."

I knew they wouldn't release me if I told them I was seeing people in color, let alone the fact that I was now also reading their thoughts and feeling their every emotion. I had already peered into the doctor's mind.

"No, all good," I replied.

He was surprised at my response; apparently, these were my first words since the accident.

"You'll let us know if you do, right?"

I nodded. He scribbled something on a pad and motioned to the nurse to return me to my room.

SIX MONTHS LATER: I was at the Grove Park Inn, having a New Year's dinner with my husband. It was the first time we'd been alone since my accident. I looked around and I could hear couples and feel couples and see couples.

"Joe?"

He looked up at me. His gaze felt different, concerned. We had been married for nine years, but over the last several months we might as well have been strangers. I'd gone from fun to serious, from social to a hermit, from spontaneous to plodder, from right brain to left brain, from egocentric to egoless.

I kept trying to explain to him, my kids, and my family: "One person went into the car and another person came out." They struggled to understand. They got frustrated when I couldn't remember past birthdays or trips or memories, so I started to pretend. My husband, to make it easier on me, started to invent a past that wasn't entirely real. It was charming and we turned it into a game. I was thankful I could remember them, at least. Now, looking into his eyes, I saw a man who waited patiently for the woman he fell in love with to return. I didn't have the heart to tell him that she never really would.

Instead, I took a deep breath and said, "I see people in color." It came out a little faster than I'd hoped. *Phew,* I thought, exhaling. *That's over with.* Actually, it was just beginning.

Chapter 11
Life in Color

"What?" Joe asked.

At first I thought I'd said it so fast he didn't hear.

I repeated, "I see people in color."

He looked confused, so I motioned towards a couple near us. "See that guy—he's red. He is stressed out about paying the bill and his girlfriend is light blue, trying to appease him." I looked back to see if Joe was getting this, but he just hung his head and sighed.

Finally, after taking a moment to compose himself, he said in a patronizing tone, "Cool." *Well at least he didn't get up and leave,* I thought. It would be years before he fully understood, before *I* fully understood, that people's colors have significance to their very souls, their very meaning of life, and their very purpose for being here—all part of a collective that sometimes sends us backward but ultimately moves us forward.

One day he asked me, "What color am I?" That's when I knew that it was beginning to resonate with him—that he had fully accepted all the spiritual shifts I was making, the work I was doing. He accepted the new me and would join me on my journey.

TODAY: You don't get to pick your superpower. At first it felt like a curse, and I would ask, "Why? Why is this happening to me?" It was overwhelming. I didn't want to know what people thought or felt or what color they were. For years I hid from my gifts, and I certainly didn't tell others about them. Then I was challenged at work and really needed to understand my team…so I peeked. I started to journal the differences in people's colors, what those colors meant, and how I could best help them in their jobs. It was amazing. Suddenly I found myself explaining colors to others and they were asking me to "read" them to help them better understand.

When I told my acupuncturist, she asked me to read her clients so she could figure out how she could best serve them. I remember one woman was shrouded in blackness and I knew that trauma from her past, and a dark entity, followed her like a black cloud. Another was indigo, the color of purpose, and was plagued with migraines.

The list goes on and on. It felt good to read people, to help people. It felt freeing. Pretty soon my friends were asking me to help them "understand" the difficult people in their lives or those they loved and wanted to be closer to. People always ask me if I am seeing their auras, but the best description I can offer is that I see their "soul color." This is different from simply observing them going about their business. If all I see of a person is that they cut me off in line, or they were harsh but truthful in their words, I am not really "seeing" them. If I really see them, I see the indigo marching towards a purpose, the red intensity of his actions, the light blue of caring no matter what. Then I am closer to understanding what this person is made of. I step into their shoes. I feel their love, their hate, their jealousy, their embarrassment, and their pain as if I was trying on a jacket or drinking a glass of water. For a moment, I wear it, or it washes over me. Carrying so much pain from my accident helped aid in developing my spiritual gifts.

As a result of this work, I stopped judging people and decided to love everyone or, at the very least, try to send them love. I started teaching empathy classes and leading workshops and testifying at women's retreats. I realized that I can tell you someone's color just from looking at their picture, and when on a hike I can sense a red or green or whatever color coming down the trail from a mile away and how many are in that group. This is handy while back-country camping in the wilds of Alaska and on the lookout for grizzlies! I can find my husband and children in a sea of people at Walmart, a stadium, or a grocery store just by reaching out and sensing where they are. And even after all this time, they ask, "How'd you know I was here?"

Once, while sitting next to my friend at a women's retreat, I accidentally answered a question she thought but did not ask out loud. She looked at me with surprise and concern. "You can read minds?"

I shrugged. "Sometimes."

I have become acutely aware that we are all connected. Sometimes our colors spill across others, our hearts connect when we are speaking or smiling at someone as they pass us on the street.

It took a long time for me to accept that this was all real and a God-given gift that is constantly growing and evolving.

We are brought here for a purpose, whether big or small, and we are kept here in some shape or form until we fulfill that purpose. We also all have gifts that we can call upon, kindness and love that we can share, and lives that we can change. My gift is seeing people in color, and using it to bring understanding and love where there was once confusion and hate. I am always surprised at how easily people accept my messages to them. No one has ever called me crazy. I hid for all those years because of my own fear and lack of acceptance. They accepted me, they saw me because they knew that for the first time, I saw them.

ABOUT THE AUTHOR: Cathy Balken is writer, angelic intuitive, empath, Usui Reiki Master, and messenger of truth. She is a visionary whose goal is to help people really "see" themselves and others, heal through compassionate connection, and find their calling. A walk-in from the angelic dimensions, Cathy regularly visits other realms for knowledge and enjoyment. She has a special relationship with seraphim, especially Rey, who she channels among other Divine Energy beings. Her strong connection to Divine Energy provides her with the abundance needed to help others.

Cathy Balken
balkencathy@gmail.com
Twitter: @seebalken

EMPATH TOOL
by Jade Rehder

Relax

The first step in this process is to determine how you organize time. Consider something fun happening in the next month or two. From what direction, in relationship to your body, does the thought come to you? Know that whatever the direction—above, below, behind, in front, or to your side—it is correct for you. This is where your future is stored, and now that you are aware of it you can do the relax practice.

Use this tool when you are creating anxiety and fear, placed in the future, about anything in your life—be it a sporting competition, meeting, or conversation with someone. You create how you are feeling (happy, sad, scared, fearful, or anxious) through what you choose to think about and the emotions generated by those thoughts on a moment-to-moment basis.

- Next, drop in to your body by doing a set of four *Let Go Breaths (see page 59),* breathing in through your nose for a count of four and out through your mouth for a count of eight. (Use this often!)

- Close your eyes.

- Imagine the desired positive outcome of what you are anxious about. What does it look, sound, and feel like for you when you have the results you have chosen? Create a full-color movie clip of it, getting as detailed as possible.

- Next, in your mind's eye, visualize floating above yourself and looking down, like you are your own personal guardian angel.

- Notice that below you there is an imagined line of time. Float out into your future toward the event you are anxious about, whichever direction that is for you.

- Now float further, to a time where what you are anxious about is complete and you have the positive result that you created in your movie clip.

- Above your line of time, turn around 180 degrees to reverse your view and face NOW.

- Notice the energy shift.

- ASK yourself, "Where is the anxiety now? Is it reduced or gone?"

- Float back to the present time, into your body, and open your eyes.

If the anxiety still has a charge, you can do this practice again until it is gone. You have now released the anxiety. You can relax. Good job!

CHAPTER 12

Never Too Late

Marisa Duran

Something woke me up. Someone clattering around in the kitchen. Yawning, I stretched and groaned, reluctant to open my eyes to the intrusion of the sun in the room. When I did try to open them, I found I couldn't. They were stuck together! I tried again, slowly stretching my eyelashes to a crack. Finally, on the third attempt, they came apart and the bedroom came into view. Bringing my hands to my eyes, I realized they were both crusted with a gooey discharge. I was about four years old.

Several years later, I asked my mother when I had an infection in my eyes. I went on to describe everything I remembered and felt that morning.

She gave me a curious look and said, "That wasn't you, that was me. I had pink eye in both eyes."

Now it was my turn to look at her strangely, because I remember the difficulty opening and looking through those infected eyes. With a shrug, it became one of those unexplained things in life that you file away. It would also be the first of several memories that flooded my mind when I was told during an akashic record reading that I might be an empath. Then in my early fifties, it was a turning point in the spiritual path I had started when I was nineteen.

The second recollection, also filed away, was of a phone call from a friend when I was twelve years old.

After the call my mother asked, "Who was that?"

"It was one of my counselors from summer camp. She just wanted someone to talk to."

Mom laughed. "What does a sixteen-year-old want with talking to a twelve-year-old?"

Again, I shrugged this off at the time. It was nothing new for someone to want to confide in me and ask me for advice, even at a young age. In fact, throughout my entire life I had spent hours and hours, on the phone and in person, listening to, empathizing with, and guiding others. When I look back at some of the advice I gave out I know it had to have come from unexplained sources. Oftentimes I was counseling on subjects I had no reference for or experience with. It was only much later that I understood why. Being an empath opens a window to how others are feeling at the time, and that ability has allowed me to soothe and provide reassuring words to everyone who calls me.

Another memory popped up, this one of a Saturday evening when my sister and I met some friends at a local steakhouse. Like many restaurants it got very busy on the weekends, and we found ourselves in a small waiting room crammed with people. The hostess announced that it would be fifteen to twenty minutes before we got a table, and since we were with friends we had no choice but to wait. As the minutes dragged on I began to feel a rising uneasiness and unexplained agitation. I had never liked being in a crowd, much less being confined in a small place with over thirty hungry people.

I leaned over to my sister and whispered, "If they don't call us soon I'm going to go and sit in the car."

She raised her eyebrows and whispered back, "Why, what's wrong?"

"My skin is literally crawling." I couldn't explain it any other way.

"Well, wait a few more minutes. Maybe they'll call us soon."

I tried putting a white light bubble around me, which helped a little while we continued to wait. Finally we were called and led into a crowded dining room. After being served our drinks and several bread baskets my angst began to wane.

I understand now that I was feeling everyone's energy and emotions in that room, including their hunger and low blood sugar. Over the years I have noticed having a low blood sugar tends to amplify one's "empathness." I know that's not a word, but it should be!

After this new piece of my puzzle began sinking in, I was a little pissed. At that time I had been on my spiritual journey for over thirty-two years, and I remember looking up at the ceiling (as we all do when we are speaking to God).

"Really, *really,* you're just now telling me this!?"

Many empaths experience anxiety, depression, and unexplained emotional rollercoasters, however, I'd never had those sorts of occurrences. I had always approached things from a logical and intellectual point of view—a detached and delayed response that spilled over into my spiritual life. Even the discovery of a new gift became a check on a list of metaphysical events. While this perspective served me well in many ways, it had caused me to miss the signs of being an empath. Even after I found a group of like-minded people, I'd start comparing my stories and encounters to theirs and realize that once again I didn't fit the mold. Why must we compare ourselves? Remember, no two people, two lives, or two journeys are alike. It took me a couple of years to get out of that mindset. The truth of who I am is enough. These days, I'm glad to be able to contribute MY point of view of MY journey.

My delayed awareness has me recalling yet another memory.

A friend and I were housesitting for other friends who owned a Christmas tree farm in Michigan. All that tree energy made it a great getaway place. The local pastor stopped by to check on us. Over some tea we talked about the weather and upcoming festivals. Then the conversation turned to relationships, and the pastor spoke of the counseling that he and his wife had started to save their marriage. My friend talked about her recent breakup. There wasn't anything different or odd about the conversation.

The pastor invited us to a service, but my friend said, "Thank you, but I really don't have time."

My response was, "You will if I slap you!"

They were both taken aback, startled at my words and the emotion behind them. I was shocked as well, and felt my heart jump. I don't normally use those words, especially not around people I don't know well.

Quickly, I sidestepped it, saying, "Oh, I'm kidding"!

I later found out the pastor and his wife were in counseling because he couldn't control his temper. I had verbally expressed his emotions!

That was the first time I felt this "gift" was an invasion of my being and soul. Being a conduit for someone's feelings, especially rage and anger, did not sit well with me. I felt out of control, intruded upon. I was just mastering my own emotions and reactions and the thought of adding someone else's to the mix was not acceptable.

Though I've certainly felt frustrated at times about what being an empath entails, I've come to realize that it is not a burden. After all, I'm the one that made the decision to step onto my path in search of answers regarding events in my life and the reason for my existence. In the process, I've learned that being an empath isn't a spoiled, unruly child. It is an open emotional spiritual window to just about everything and even though we can't control it, we can prepare ourselves. As you explore this ability and incredible aspect of yourself, you'll begin to realize that you are a beacon for all kinds of energy, both negative and positive. This is a responsibility that requires a certain level of maturity, which means you will have to make adjustments to your everyday routine in order to create a balance in your life. In this way it is like many milestones such as marriage, parenthood, caring for an elderly parent, and even retirement, all of which prompts us to adapt so we can stay sane.

Chapter 12
Never Too Late

The key is to have patience with ourselves.

You will also need to establish new daily protections and clearings, and sometimes invoke and request help from your guides and angels—who I affectionately call "my team." Establish a connection with your own team. Talk to them, ask them for help, even if you can't hear them yet. Remember, we all have free will, so they are not allowed to step in unless we request it. I usually begin my day with the four S's: shit, shower, shave, and shield. Like an umbrella on a rainy day, protection will be very helpful in warding off other people's energy and emotions.

First, imagine a white bubble engulfing your entire body. Sit with that a minute. Notice big or subtle changes. How does it affect you? Has it lessened your anxiety? Do you feel calmer? Now, over the years I have had to add another layer of protection over me, my home, and family, which I do by asking my angels, deceased loved ones, and even Archangels, in the form of a prayer similar to this one:

"With the protection of my team and angels, with the protection of all the Archangels, with the protection of all ascended masters, no malevolent, dark, earthbound souls or entities are allowed here, around me, in me, or in the house or through my phone. You're not allowed. I send you off with light and love, and may you begin your awakening toward the light. God bless you, God bless you, God bless you. Amen."

Of course, you can make changes that are comfortable for you and your beliefs. This daily habit can make life and heavy emotional situations a little easier to weather.

Second, when the emotions and energy become too overwhelming, just put the brakes on. We are always rushing and never take the time for ourselves. Begin by asking yourself, "Are these my emotions, or someone else's?" Pay attention to your body and mind's response when you ask yourself that question. Does your anxiety automatically ease when you ask if it's someone else's? If so, you're on the way to defusing the sensations you're experiencing rather than spiraling into an emotional mess. I can tell you from personal experience that nine times out of ten you'll find that what you are feeling does not belong to you.

When I'm picking up other people's "stuff," my next step is to take a moment to ground myself so I can slow down any impending meltdowns. Grounding yourself consists of imagining your legs growing into roots that extend down into the soil to the center of the earth. It creates a soothing exchange of energies while anchoring yourself and stabilizing what you are feeling. I always thank Mother Earth for helping me ground myself.

Finally. I take an hour every day to meditate. Just for one hour, put yourself first and have that timeout. It's a way of giving your body, mind, and spirit a reset. If I'm sick I will do an extra hour of meditation in the evening. There are many forms of meditation. Explore them all and choose what speaks to you, your body, and soul.

When I first began meditating I had a very hectic schedule that included working sixty-plus hours a week. So I started slow—just one hour a week—using a Chakra CD I had purchased. Chakras are invisible energy spots throughout the body that can get clogged or closed by past traumas or negative energy. As I incorporated this "break" for myself, I slowly began experiencing subtle changes in my body, health and, surprisingly, my temperament. Over time I bumped it to two times a week, then to every day. I do want to take this time to thank my sister for moving in with me, which pushed me to meditate EVERY day.

I have been told by many people that they can't meditate because they fall asleep or are too antsy to focus. First of all, one reason you are meditating is in fact to get rid of that "antsyness." Second, your subconscious, body, and soul are always listening, even when you're asleep. As you get into the habit of taking this time for yourself, you can always add a more focused or lengthy meditation, if you choose. Remember, you're just making the time to get to know yourself and help find some balance in your ever-evolving life. Most importantly, don't forget to be gentle with yourself as you would with a friend or loved one.

It has been my honor to share some of my experiences with you. I know that incorporating these tools into your daily routine will help you ride the wave as you embrace your empathic abilities and continue discovering new spiritual gifts with more joy and ease.

ABOUT THE AUTHOR: Marisa Duran is a writer and Capricornian Empath who began her spiritual journey over thirty-eight years ago. She has spent the last three decades discovering and developing her gifts, which has allowed her to assist others in overcoming their obstacles and exploring their own unique abilities in a safe space. A Capricorn at heart, Marisa draws on her natural patience to guide and profoundly change the way others view themselves, their path, and the way they relate to people in their lives. Many have said upon hearing her voice they are instantly put at ease. Now retired, Marisa enjoyed a thirty-one-year career at AT&T and spends her time reading and geocaching.

Marisa Duran
marisaduran101@gmail.com

EMPATH TOOL
by Jade Rehder

It's Time to Thank Yourself!

How often each day do you say "Thank you"—be it to friends, family, the barista who makes your coffee, or a customer service person who helps you with a computer issue? It may be five, ten, maybe even more if you count emails to colleagues. Now ask yourself, how many times do you say, "Thank you" to yourself?

Your inner control system (also known as your body/mind) listens to everything you say and think. It also stores your memories and is the level of mind at which learning and change happen— through repetition and processes, by easy-to-understand statements and commands. Each time you thank yourself, you are offering encouragement to the body/mind in support of a positive mindset, habits, and behaviors; therefore, the more you do this, the more you will like what is occurring in your life.

- Start by observing when you say "Thank you" to others. Notice how you feel.

- Now, notice when your body/mind assists you in your day. When you are changing a habit, such as biting your nails, thank yourself for reminding you to stop. Do this every time you catch the behavior, and you will be amazed by how quickly you can create change.

- Thank yourself while driving, for example, when you are distracted and look up just in time to stop safely or want to change lanes and get that reminder to look again just as a speeding vehicle pulls into that lane.

- Say Thank You to Yourself often, ideally several times a day, whenever you want to support and reinforce what you would like to experience more of.

- With regular practice, you will find that you more easily remember things and find misplaced items just by asking yourself where they are located.

- You are expanding your internal awareness and trust muscle to create a deeper connection between your linear cognitive mind and body/mind.

CHAPTER 13

Trusting Light, Trusting You
Deborah Reid

I have spent weeks in excitement and fear of publicly writing this chapter. This is version six, as it has taken me a while to figure out how to describe what it has felt like to be me, with multiple lives rolled into one. Having lived in thirty-four residences in multiple states, I consider myself a gypsy, forever seeking the next great adventure!

Even as a young child I felt different from the others in my traditional middle-class household. Though my knowledge of God was limited to the name I prayed to over food and before bed, I had "experiences" that the people in my life did not believe. This earned me the name "Dippy Debbie" because I was so sensitive and thought of as having my head in the clouds. The first of these experiences occurred at age seven when, during a stressful event, I was visited by an "invisible friend" who turned out to be my deceased grandfather watching over me and keeping me safe.

Then, at the age of eleven, I learned that God was more than just something I prayed to. I remember begging to fly away with the birds who had not a care in the world, and suddenly there I was—out of my body and flying! I knew then that wherever and whatever God was, He/She/It heard me, and responded. I would never be alone. After that experience, I wanted more! I craved knowledge; I questioned everything in life, and I wanted to understand why things were the way they were. Why couldn't we take the hobo man home for Thanksgiving dinner? I could feel his loneliness and we had plenty, so why couldn't we share? And because I did not find the answers in my external world, I turned inward and was given them by that clear, gender-neutral voice I heard. Sometimes I would say, "I need You to tell me three times, so I know it is You," and She/He/It did. Sometimes it was in a song, a stranger's voice or nod, or on a billboard! I would laugh, thinking *What a sense of humor!* Over time, the voice became an instant knowing, and when I didn't listen, there were experiences I preferred not to have had. When I did listen, however, I continued to get guidance that helped me, comforted me, protected me, and amazed me! This was a gradual, step-by-step process that occurred over many years.

I did not understand I was an empath until I felt something stab my head as I walked down a hospital corridor while visiting my dad. A nurse near a window heard me cry out and said, "Oh, I have a migraine too." When I got in the elevator, I intuitively said, "If this is not mine, please take it away." Boom—it was gone instantly—leaving me pain-free and elated.

I did not know I could be a conduit for healing until the energy began coming out of my hands. I am now a Reiki Master/Teacher, but I was first taught by Spirit. This is still evolving.

I did not know I was a medical intuitive until I saw cancer inside a person who had cancer.

I questioned if angels were real, then I saw my first of many. I learned they are here to assist us.

I questioned string theory (the idea that everything is linked by minuscule, energetic strings) until God showed me that we are indeed connected, heart to heart, through this amazing light! At the time I had begun learning about quantum physics, and I asked God to show me if this is real and how it works. An hour later, I was in a Costco parking lot when suddenly I saw a light beam going from one person's heart to another's! It was true! And I did not understand energy fields or really believe in vortex openings until I began to see them, oddly hanging in the air, as I sat in open-eye meditations. I just observed, and then, as I got comfortable, they grew bigger, from small portals to toroidal fields.

I did not know I could receive Light codes until I saw them being written in my own body after asking, during a meditation, to receive permanent muscle healing from pain.

I did not know I could give a reading until I tried. It is amazing how when you learn to "seek and you will find," the answers "shall be given!"

I did not know I was a medium until I began communicating with loved ones of mine and others after their physical deaths. I love this connection!

I did not understand about heaven until I died in 1983. After that, I spent a great deal of time talking to pastors, ministers, and clergy of all denominations as to why it was not what they said. It took sixteen years before I found a Methodist minister who believed me!

And finally, I did not truly understand Jesus until I met Him. I had prayed for this understanding all my life; then, while I was in my friend's yard one morning, deeply praying and asking for guidance about a medical choice I had to make, He appeared—my teacher, my brother, my friend, standing there in broad daylight! During this conversation I asked Him many questions, like, is it true that we can do all the things He did? (He said yes.) Why hadn't I seen Him when I died? Was this why I was dying again? He was very clear in all His answers, and when I told him I needed a teacher who only spoke the truth (the churches hadn't helped me), He offered this suggestion: *"Try reading only the words in red in your Bible, as they haven't changed them too much. Read them as if I am talking to you directly in conversation."* He also promised me I would be healed, though for larger reasons, and the sake of other people, I would have to endure a medical process. I did, and I was healed. Nothing we do only affects us, period. We are all connected through this great loving light of the Alpha and Omega.

Even as I was having these incredible supernatural experiences, my physical life was often an ongoing battle. Often, I would "put it away" and try to be like others. I refused to be molded into anyone else's idea of who I should be, yet I thought I needed to be less. With this, I created a great deal of struggle and emotional suffering. I often put myself in situations in friendship and in love that I shouldn't have.

I rescued everyone for the first twenty-five years of my life. My heart always felt another's feelings and knew I could help them. This was often to my own detriment; my life came second to others, then, after my first child, it came third. I didn't know what boundaries were, let alone how to create them. The exception was at my job, where I just followed the rules as I had been taught. Otherwise, I had only *one* rule: when someone else is hurting or feeling lost, lonely, or depressed, you help them. Their needs then came before my own, and I always had plenty to share, until I did NOT. This forced me to finally create my own boundaries and stop rescuing people.

In 2013, another major life change came in the form of a hit-and-run drunk driving accident that left me with muscular shock/trauma lockdown, no reflexes, Thoracic Outlet Syndrome, Traumatic Brain Injury (TBI), and epilepsy. Gone were many memories and the abilities to read, write, and organize in the mind or in life. One-step processing became my normal. I had worked with money my whole adult life, now I couldn't even count it. I lost my balance and could no longer cook, clean, or walk steadily. Any fluorescent lighting shut my brain down, making it very difficult to shop. I gave up my business and struggled to complete paperwork for my husband's business. I lost my license.

Before the accident, I had never been busier or happier. I had found and been married to the love of my life for twenty-one years. I ran his business and mine, and we had raised one child, with two more in high school. My heart was full, living the dream life we had created, one in which complete love and acceptance was given and returned. He knew my all, I knew his all, and we were truly soulmates. He encouraged me to reveal my gifts to the world, and in fact I had just left a channeling group and was on my way home when the accident happened.

Afterward, I felt like a shell of my former self—lost, scared, and, most days, unable to hold a train of thought. For the first three years we marveled at the way the right doctor, specialist, or alternative healing came as needed. We also walked away from every doctor who said my condition was permanent. This was not easy in any way, and I cried a lot when alone, often asking why I couldn't get the miraculous healing I knew was possible. Through it all we trusted, and some days were easier than others. Despite the challenges, we trusted, knowing it would be fine one day; we were in it together.

When I confessed to my husband that I could not read anymore, he took me to the mountains for the weekend where I read elementary school books repeatedly, all the way up to a middle school book that belonged to our daughter. I just thought if I could get the brain to remember, everything would fall into place—and I was right! On Sunday afternoon I finally was able to read again! We celebrated each step!

Fascinated, I began studying every body part and how the neurological and muscular systems work—first by reading medical books, then "seeing" it and feeling the personal experience. In 2016, just days after our first vacation in three years and when my path to healing seemed clear, my beloved had a double heart attack and left earth. In that one second, everything in my life changed again. Still unable to function at a "normal" adult level, I now felt more lost and broken than ever. Completely devastated, I was lying in bed one night and decided to try to "leave." This was not a suicide attempt; I just wanted to exit my body and go be with him. I did, but was sent back. It was not my time.

That was five years ago, and my beloved continues to speak with me, as he has since the morning after he left his body. Truly, love never dies! How I do it is by relying on God/Source/Spirit first. It's an ongoing heart-brain and higher conversation that occurs all the time.

Each of us has our own unique path, like our fingerprints. This world is changing rapidly now, and we were all born for this time, and everything is perfectly in alignment. Language is inadequate to describe the depth of this knowing, but what I hope you take from my story, above all else, is to trust. Trust yourself, and trust what you feel. Follow it through, knowing we are never alone.

Connect with your Source every day and allow your relationship with He/She/It to grow and flourish. Connect with a friend or another empath if needed. Connect with me if you feel a desire to do so. We all need human connections in which we can be ourselves and sometimes share our remarkable gifts and experiences with someone who believes us. That said, if you choose or need to keep it to yourself, do so, for soon many more will join us.

Always choose love. Trust what you are given, even if it is beyond your current awareness, and be grateful, for everything that occurs is but a thread of what is truly out there to know and experience. Take time to play! And, most importantly, remember to be you, living from the heart in everything you do!

ABOUT THE AUTHOR: Deborah Reid is currently a circle leader and medical intuitive with multifaceted gifts as a Reiki Master/ Teacher, Akashic guide/reader, clairvoyant, and medium. She refers to herself as a Christian Mystic, expanded by the love of the divine Christ Consciousness she embodies. She does not like the boxes or titles we give ourselves for these abilities—they are all aspects of our original selves. She revels in helping Christians to stay out of fear when a divine shift occurs. Deb respects and works with the many paths to God/Source/Spirit and sees the connections that unite us all. Deb has been "open" for fifty-four years and professionally assisting others since 2001 while continuing her own evolutionary journey and self-healing.

Deborah (Deb) Reid
3wayliving@gmail.com
Find me on Facebook: Deb Reid

Unwritten

Have you ever thought about how "on purpose" you live each day? If you are like many of us, the alarm goes off and the list of to-dos immediately starts running in your head. You get out of bed and life just happens minute by minute. It's like someone else is driving the bus (your life) and on a route that you don't know.

You have a choice for every action, no matter how large or small! Some ways in which you can make those choices consciously is through prayer, meditation, stretching, or the Unwritten practice below.

- Start your day by sitting up in bed.

- Close your eyes.

- Create a visual image for each event, occurrence, and connection you want in your day. Invite it in!

- Have something to do today that you would rather avoid? Remember to practice the "Let Go" breath (See page 59) until you feel your energy shift.

- Feel what it is like to enjoy your day. You are writing the song of your day before you sing it.

- Have a long to-do list? Picture asking for the support you need to accomplish your list, then allow the Universe to do its work. One morning I had twenty-seven things on my list, and within a few hours twenty-two of those things were completed, thanks to the right people showing up at a meeting and sending me emails, voicemails, and text messages with the information I needed. As a result of using this practice to imagine easily accomplishing my tasks *and* having time to breathe, what had looked like a day of overwhelming tasks flipped and became a day of spaciousness.

• Remember to ask for what you want to invite into your day!

CHAPTER 14

The Empath and The Narcissist
It Doesn't Go Well, But It Ends Well
Myrna James

I cried all the way to my wedding, and they were not "happy tears." It was a few days before the big day, and my fiancé and I were making the three-hour drive from Denver to Steamboat Springs to meet up with friends and family coming from all over the world to celebrate with us in the snowy mountains. Everything was ready, from the small quaint stone chapel, to the platinum rings to signify our love, to the breathtaking gown with fur around the neckline and sparkly jewels on the bodice. Truly, I couldn't think of a more perfect setting to make the most important promise of my life. And yet...

As we wove our way through the glorious winter-white evergreens, something deep inside me knew that this was not right. It was my own knowing, my intuition, my deep subconscious, which I have learned is always for my greater good. I now think of that inner knowing as my higher self, the one who always has my back, but it's much more than that. My higher self is connected to God. She's the part of me that's truly Divine.

Since my higher self knew something that my mind could not consciously comprehend, she found another way to convey this very important message: through my physical body. Frankly, I had been getting these "warnings" for months. I didn't feel inner peace or happiness; I felt like something was wrong. I'd even kidnapped my fiancé for a weekend to have a "come to Jesus" conversation about whether we should do this. Today, I could still drive you straight to that coffee shop where, armed with a long list of things to address, I grilled him. Somehow, he passed that test!

The truth was, he passed because I let him pass. I wanted to get married…and I wanted it *now*, to *this* man.

So my mind continued to rationalize it. And that's how I found. myself, despite three hours of confusing crying in the car, vowing to become his partner for life. I will admit that several awkward moments and red flags occurred that weekend, but I still couldn't acknowledge it to myself. At the time, I attributed it to having "cold feet."

It would take several years, and many more clues of discomfort from my body, before I could accept the truth of our relationship. And, after buying a home, solidifying our careers, and adopting our son, I finally realized I had to leave.

I was devastated. He was furious. Our son was three.

I learned that my husband is probably a narcissist—a personality type that can be so subtle it's hard to discern. I also learned about my part in our dynamic, and just how toxic it was for me.

Many empaths know about the Empath-Narcissist connection. Empaths are targets for narcissists (unconsciously) because we often put others' feelings, priorities, wants, and needs before our own—at least we do so before we learn to protect our energy and add healthy boundaries. Sometimes empaths are codependent as well. Narcissists are the opposite: their own needs come first, usually at the expense of the other. Again, it's subtle but very important.

To help visualize this, I think about these categories along a horizontal "Personality Continuum." Picture right in the middle a place of healthy confidence, where most of us want to be. To the left of this sliding scale is lower self-esteem—and we all go there sometimes in some areas of our lives. Moving along this invisible line to the right and past the place of confidence is narcissism. Moving further right, we come to places for sociopaths and psychopaths, whose personalities cause harm to others in more obvious ways. We all move along this continuum to some degree, but foundationally, we are rooted in the place where our personalities formed as children, for better or worse.

The confident middle is the healthy place. Being more left or right is unhealthy. The difference between left (low self-esteem and putting others first at the expense of self) and right (putting the self first at the expense of others) is that those on the left normally *want* to change. They want to become healthier and more confident. Those on the right are mostly oblivious. They rarely see that they are living their entire lives from an unhealthy place, and if others point it out, they will deny it vehemently. A key factor here is that they often do not feel enough emotional pain themselves, or enough empathy for those they are hurting, to change.

On a practical level, here are a few ways to help you figure out if you're with a narcissist. It's far more complex than noticing that they are selfish. One giveaway is that they rarely take responsibility for problems or mistakes. In a discussion, they will deflect blame back to you by saying it was your fault, or completely change the subject to something that *was* your fault, all to throw you off balance. Another way to deflect the conversation away from their mistake is to just talk around it, making no sense. This ends up gaslighting you, creating a confusing, horrific psychological state where you start to think that you're going crazy.

Anger was my brand of "crazy," and led me to do things that were completely out of character. And get this: narcissists *enjoy* making you crazy! They get a perverse pleasure watching the bad behavior, without taking responsibility for having somewhat caused it.

Dr. Christiane Northrup notes in her book, *Dodging Energy Vampires*, that this confusion creates cognitive dissonance in the mind; you literally cannot think straight. And long-term cognitive dissonance leads to illness due to the increased levels of cortisol (the stress hormone) and chronic inflammation over time. For me, this manifested as a life-long thyroid condition.

You also spend hours and hours trying to figure out what just happened, because it made no sense. I'd analyze and overanalyze what we'd said in an argument, trying to figure out when and why it went off the rails, picking apart every word in an effort to wrap my head around it. Then I'd send long emails to him, painstakingly trying to make my point—all the while making sure to acknowledge that I was aware I had issues too and was happy to address them at another time.

Are we victims? Yes, in a way, but we must still take responsibility for our own lives and "do the work" of becoming as healthy as possible in this lifetime. I know this because it was the specific shadow work I had to do in subsequent years. It was only through painfully tearing open the scabs in my own heart and psyche, bleeding blood-red again, that my wounds healed into beautiful scars—which are now hidden and treasured badges of honor.

As mentioned, codependency is common for empaths, including those who partner with narcissists. In a nutshell, being with the other—and putting their happiness before our own—is how we get our self-worth. I was always so proud to be with my ex because he's so confident and unique. His presence commands attention when he walks into a room, and I loved being his woman, even after our divorce when we were still "friends for the sake of our son." I now have this presence within myself (and did for years prior to this unhealthy relationship), and don't need to gain this type of affirmation externally.

What did I learn? Well, *everything*. This will give you an idea:

1. I listen to my body. It doesn't lie. It's my higher self trying to tell me something. Those goosebumps mean truth. That fluttering in my heart, the butterflies, means pay attention

to the person I'm with. The truth resonates at a higher frequency, and those vibrations are truth resonating in my body.

2. Psychology is very important. I'm learning the subtle signs of unhealthy people and paying attention.

3. I've healed my emotional pain. There are so many ways to do so, and I've done them all: talk therapy, Soul Sister women's groups, yoga, meditation, hypnosis, past life regressions, retreats, and so on.

4. I listen to the whispers of my intuition for what I need to know, or what to do next. This requires clearing the mind of the noise, of the chatter of our egos. To quiet the "Monkey Mind," I meditate using a mantra, get totally present by taking a long hot shower, walk along a river or in the forest listening to the flow of nature…This is when the messages come through. Meditation does not have to mean sitting quietly and feeling guilty that we keep having thoughts.

5. Set boundaries. "Boundaries are the distance at which I can love you and me simultaneously," noted Prentis Hemphill.

As we listen for the whispers of our intuition, it helps to know that the voices in our heads are not actually us—for we are the ones *listening* to the voices in our heads, as Michael Singer points out in his epic book, *The Untethered Soul*. This means that the voice is not always right! Sometimes it's our ego, trying to protect us from harm. Or it's our inner child, making sure we don't get hurt again. It's usually not good to act from the words coming from these parts of us. The beautiful thing is that as we raise our own conscious awareness, that voice automatically becomes that of our higher selves for more minutes of the day, over time and with effort.

This is not easy, living in the 3D world. We have to pay the mortgage and feed the kids, all while navigating these subtle energies and personality issues.

I like to think of it as in the film *The Matrix*, where we can choose the blue pill and remain stuck in an unconscious way of living, or we can choose the red pill and start living from truth. The latter may be harder—digging at our inner child's scars, feeling the pain all over again so they can heal properly—but the alternative is to continue making decisions from that unhealed wounded place, or from other unconscious aspects, and wondering where our lives have gone wrong.

I didn't believe in destiny until I had my astrological natal chart read. Seeing my life mapped out in that way made me believe that we each have a divine path. But the thing is, it's only visible to us if we heal our wounds and learn to follow that inner guidance— because that is the voice of God. And God has a plan to take us down this divine path, if we can just get out of our own way. I'm finally getting there.

Now, twenty years later, I find myself crying again—and this time, it's tears of joy. I'm with my ex and our son and a glass of beautiful red wine in a booth at a steakhouse (one of our traditions). It's tears of gratitude for all that I have in my life because of this relationship. Through my tears, I thank him. I have a son; I never would have adopted him without a partner. I have the wisdom from this process and a much deeper path of personal growth. And I still have him—as a co-parent and friend, he's solid and reliable, someone I can count on, and I'm so grateful.

Join me at Soulful Vibrant Living as we move down the path from confusion and unconsciousness into awareness and light. One tiny light dispels all the darkness around. Let's bring that light, for ourselves and for each other.

Chapter 14
The Empath and The Narcissist

ABOUT THE AUTHOR: Myrna is a journalist and publisher who explores the nexus of science and spirituality. The publication she has owned for two decades, *Apogeo Spatial*, is about the importance of data—location, Earth science, and data used for training Artificial Intelligence (AI) algorithms. Her current work focuses on the importance of ethics in AI, and on the power of a broader worldview, such as seeing Earth from space. After a decade in Chicago of managing national accounts like Nikon, Sony, and Procter and Gamble for national magazines, she spent 1998 and 1999 traveling the world solo and blogging on her live travel website before "blogging" was even a word. She lives in Denver with her amazing adopted autistic son.

Myrna James
myrna@soulfulvibrantliving.com
SoulfulVibrantLiving.com
ApogeoSpatial.com
BluelinePublishingLLC.com

Words Create Your World

Do you ever stop to consider the power of the words you use and hear every day? Remember when you were very young and someone told you "No!"? How did it make you feel? You can still easily access the feeling today.

Understanding the way your subconscious mind processes words is imperative. If I say, "Don't picture Mickey Mouse," you find you have a very clear picture of that famous mouse in your mind's eye. This is because your subconscious mind is unable to process negatives and instead creates a picture that matches the words, minus those negatives. When you use the words "can't," "don't," "not," or any other word that negates, your subconscious mind naturally filters them out and only hears the rest of the information. This also applies to statements you make about what you don't want. You create that picture and start bringing it into your life. Your vibrations match the words you use.

- Choose a day, ideally today!

- Your challenge is to observe how words create results, reactions, behavior, and feelings, thus creating your world.

- You will begin to notice the impact of your words on other people.

- Just watch your words land on the other person. How does their facial expression shift? Does their color change? What is their body language saying to you?

- Then you will begin to notice the effect of others' words on you.

- What feelings are created within you?

- You have the power to be at choice with your reaction or response.

- Notice what you are creating when you use negations in your words. Remember?

- This awareness makes it much easier to intentionally allow Words to Create Your World.

Take the practice further and notice how you react to the words of the music you listen to. What do you feel inside when you listen? What is your response to what you read? How about the stories you watch in movies or on television? Are the pictures you are creating and the feelings being emanated in your body bringing you closer to what you want in your life?

Words create everyone's world very quickly. This is why it is so important that everything you think and say is as intentional as possible. Creating harmony with God/Universe/Source, yourself, and with others becomes easier when you are consciously using your words and thoughts!

CHAPTER 15

When I am Fifty, I Want to Be You

Iris Sadeh Rosler

The first word I knew in Spanish was *bruja*, or witch. Growing up in Israel, Hebrew was my primary language and English, my second; Spanish was my parents' secret language for talking to each other—especially about us girls. Whenever I heard the word *bruja*, I knew they were referring to me—and likely saying I'd been mean to my younger sister again. I remember listening by the closed bedroom door as they used the dreaded word, adding that I could sense my sister's vulnerabilities and "play" with them. I also remember how my body started to ache and how my soul felt like a squashed cockroach.

"I am a good girl," I wanted to shout, "not a witch!"

I was six years old.

The next night, from my spot by the door, I heard them elaborate further, saying that I could "feel" people's difficulties.

I could not stand it anymore. What was wrong with me? Why couldn't I be a normal girl? I didn't want to be a bruja; I wanted to be a fairy! So sad and disappointed in myself, I had no idea that I would one day not only embrace being a "witch," but it would become the main meaning of my life.

Most of my childhood memories are connected to playing outside, games like "Hide and Seek"; "Catches"; and others we invented that involved mostly running and catching. When we got older, we would create or copy special dances for popular songs and perform them on a made-up stage in the playground. Each afternoon, my sister and I would do our homework, all the while stealing glances at the clock. Then, at four p.m. on the dot, we would race out of our small apartment to the shared grass between the buildings to play with the neighbors' children. It was only when the sun went down that we reluctantly dragged ourselves back inside. Most of the time I knew my friends' thoughts and feelings. I sometimes told them this, but it did not seem to matter; we simply went on playing or dancing. No one cared that I was a witch, which I greatly appreciated. I also liked being able to share this information with them.

My sister and I were champions at jumping rope, tree climbing, dancing, and handstands. I especially loved hanging upside-down on the playground ladder and seeing the sky under me—sometimes blue and beautiful, other times gray and foggy—and the ground, along with trees, houses, and people, above. Almost fifty years have passed, yet the feeling remains vivid! My mind is like a baby, wrapped in its favorite blanket and lying in a crib; it is clear.

Everything changed my last year of elementary school. After six weeks at home recovering from a broken arm, I returned to school excited to be around my friends again. Instead, I felt like a stranger, with no one looking or talking to me. It took me a good half an hour to realize I was being deliberately shunned. I sat there, my stomach contracted as if someone had stuck a newspaper with glue in it, until the middle of the day when I ran home and crawled into bed. All I wanted was to get under my blanket and wake up when it was alright to be me—not like everyone else, but special, a *bruja*. I never found out why I was shunned, though looking back I imagine that I "saw" too many things about my classmates and was not sensitive enough with the information.

As high school approached I decided that I needed to become serious—no more playing, no more spending time outside. My life would now be focused on books and what I considered to be "grown-up" pursuits, which in my mind were connected to being inside and sitting on a chair. My hard work paid off and, after taking a very long test I was accepted to Jerusalem's most prestigious high school. I still remember the excitement and pride when I opened the letter addressed to me and saw those three words: "You are accepted." I was jumping for joy, convinced that the rest of my life would be different. I also remember that my good friend did not pass the test, and how I felt her disappointment even more than my joy, so much so that it almost drained my hope for a better future.

That said, life did improve when I went to high school. I don't recall much about the academics, though I am sure they were rigorous. However, I do have vivid memories of being in the dancing ensemble and being a leader in the scouts. Dancing, being with friends who accepted me, and hiking in nature evoked a similar feeling to when my sister and I played—I felt like time stopped and raced at the same time, and my body felt like a feather flying in the air—so light and carefree. During high school I started knowing what I was meant to do—or at least my body knew it. My mind still did not accept it.

By the time I turned twenty-one, I was terrified. I had my high school diploma and had served three years in the Israeli army, followed by a short trip to Europe with my boyfriend, but I had no idea what I wanted to do with my life. Since I have always been about forward movement and searching for my inner truth, I decided to enroll at university. I would continue studying on and off for many years, mostly social sciences, and though I loved all the new ideas I was still disconnected from myself. I also got married, and thankfully knew enough to never take this relationship for granted, consciously deciding every year to stay together, happily or not. My love and I took the journey together, passing the good and the bad of life, respecting each other's choices even when we didn't necessarily agree with them, and welcoming changes to our lives independently and together.

Most importantly, he knew and accepted that I was a witch. Being connected so deeply to my life partner enabled my soul to be curious, independent, and fresh; it also made me very optimistic about the possibility of finding my life purpose, which had continued to elude me. In my mind, serious people did serious work—meaning they were doctors like my father, teachers like my mother, therapists like my mother-in-law, and academics like my man. It was always indoors and connected to talking and thinking. Not in a million years did I think I would be working outside, and bringing my great gift to the world.

It wasn't until I turned forty that I finally discovered what my life purpose was, and the age of fifty when I could define and pursue it—this, after I met my mentor Tim Kelley and studied the True Purpose method. It changed my life, and I could not believe my good fortune.

Yet this realization was devastating as well. I was a mess thinking of all the lost years I'd felt incomplete and not aligned with myself. I hated myself for wanting to be this person who works in an office, wears a suit, drives a company car, and talks for a living, when the real key to my self-fulfillment had been there since I was a young girl. How did I not know myself?

At the same time, I was flying high with happiness and relief that after so many years I could finally be myself—a *bruja*. Finding my purpose made it possible for me to wake up every morning with vitality and happiness. Suddenly, it was easy for me to be free with my senses and use them wisely. I was a "good witch"—a fairy. My sense of smell became heightened; when I woke up in the morning coffee smelled like love; all bread smelled like my grandmother's home; soup felt safe; and soap smelled pure. My senses now ran the show—no drugs, all natural—and it was normal for me. My purpose was a combination of my *essence* (happiness, beauty, and love) and my *blessing* (my abilities as a *bruja*), manifested as enabling leaders to be the best version of themselves. This was the gift I needed to bring to the world.

In the beginning, I did not know how I was going to fulfill this purpose, but for the first time in my life I trusted the process and was willing to be flexible and vulnerable. The years of futile searching had taken their toll on my body in the form of high blood pressure and shallow breathing. At the age of forty-seven I took my first yoga class, and it was the beginning of reconnecting to my body in a soft, considerate, and feminine way. Slowly I found my breath again and, like a newborn coming to the world, I practiced it gently, enjoying and playing with the inhale and exhale. Yoga would be a journey in and of itself, which eventually led to my becoming a teacher. One of my challenges during training was to stand on my head for one hundred breaths. Somewhere around the fortieth breath, it came to me: that wonderful baby-in-a-cozy-blanket feeling I'd felt as a kid. A range of unexpected emotions, including happiness and even fear—flowed through me, but mostly I just felt whole.

Once my body was aligned and I got into a routine of keeping connected to it, I had the energy, humility, and freedom to find how was I going to be a practicing *bruja*. What did I need to do to combine my purpose with my gift?

"When the student is ready, the teacher will appear," says the Buddha. When I was connected and ready, another mentor showed up, in the form of Nilima Bhat, who showed me the path to studying Shakti Leadership. With my mentors and other soulmates as guides and fellow travelers, I took a big, brave journey into myself and my own leadership style, letting my witch qualities shine and never sweeping past wounds under the rug. I had always been able to "see" people, now it was time to help them shine.

In celebration of my fifty-fifth birthday, my friend and I braved the pandemic to travel from Israel to Denver to relax and recharge.

After spending quality time with some other friends, we drove a cool Jeep up to the mountains in search of adventure. I will never forget the incredible feeling of resting my body in the Glenwood hot springs, the red Rocky Mountains on my one side and my good friend on the other; snowflakes were flying above us. *Life is so good,* I thought, *We are whole, free, fulfilled, happy, and creative.* Sitting with us in the pool were two lovely women in their twenties, both from India. Shia was a doctor starting her specialization in pediatrics, and her best friend, Lakshmi, was an engineer who had just moved to Denver for a new job. As we spoke, I marveled at these beautiful souls, thinking of their great courage at being so far from home and from their families. They had been raised on the same principles as I and had worked very hard to become who they were today.

"What are you doing in life?" Shia asked.

"I am a mentor," I replied, "I enable leaders to be the best version of themselves, using their senses."

Shia's expression was one of puzzlement and curiosity. "Iris, how do you do it?"

"I help them connect to their bodies, to their souls, and then to their career and purpose. I work mostly outdoors, and in groups. After going through the journey by myself I know it is easier to have a coach; however, the transformation is individual and it changes their lives."

We continued talking about our lives and how covid had changed them, but I noticed that Shia seemed lost in thought. Before leaving, she whispered to me, "When I am fifty, I want to be you!"

As I smiled at her I realized my face was wet, but not from the snow or the hot springs. They were tears of the free-flowing joy that comes from living as the authentic, loving *bruja* I was always meant to be.

ABOUT THE AUTHOR: Iris Sadeh Rosler is an organizational consultant, True Purpose coach, Tiara Leadership Coach, and facilitator who has spent the last twenty years enabling leaders and teams to bring themselves more fully to their professional and personal lives. Iris personally coaches leaders and leads workshops and outdoor special retreats for upper management. A pioneer in Shakti leadership in Israel, Iris uses a variety of new and unique methods in creating and facilitating initiatives on such topics as women's leadership, empowerment, resiliency, authenticity, and conscious leadership. Iris loves dancing, practicing and teaching yoga, and hiking with her family.

Iris Sadeh Rosler
Conscious Leadership
linkedin.com/in/iris-sadeh-rosler-סיריא-הדש-רלֹסר-1b765a10b
Irissadeh@gmail.com
+1972542888691

Rehearsing

You have probably heard about the benefits of setting intentions for your day. Did you know that you can more easily activate these intentions through rehearsing? Remember when you were in school and you were acting in a play or played a musical instrument for a recital? You had a number of rehearsals so you knew what you wanted to do in the production, right? Well, you can do the same with any situation or interaction in your life.

Rehearsing also creates flow in your day.

- Start with a simple event like going to the grocery store or driving somewhere.

- Envision how you want the experience to play out.

- Be very specific, remembering each step and ASKing for it to play out the way you desire.

- If you are working on rehearsing a conversation with someone, remember you are at choice to react or respond. If you believe they may be upset by what you have to say, rehearse how you will respond. This sets the energy up for you to be calm and centered no matter how the other person responds, and use all your tools with more ease.

You can rehearse anything in your life because you are always co-creating. Rehearse, rehearse, and rehearse!

CHAPTER 16

Who Runs the World

Elisa Tawil

D o you know why a marathon is 26.2 miles? I'll admit that I had no idea in 2012 when I began training to be a runner. In fact, I didn't give it any thought at all; I was focused on my goal of running the New York City Marathon when I turned thirty.

Running competitions are very popular in my home city of São Paulo, Brazil. With a population of nearly twenty-two million people, São Paulo is the largest city in the country and the fourth-largest in the world. It also has several beautiful landmarks, around which the routes of these competitions are usually centered. That year, 2012, was my first time competing in a ten-kilometer race. By the final stretch, I was exhausted and thinking about just walking to the finish line. That's when I looked beside me and happened to lock eyes with a woman I hadn't noticed before. "Let's do it together," she said, giving me the incentive and the energy to keep on running to the end.

To me, that moment of connection between us symbolizes what it means to embody and practice empathy. You don't need to know the other person; you just need to know yourself and from this place you are able to provide support and encouragement.

It would take several years, motherhood, and several professional challenges before I was able to fully step into this knowledge of self and my gifts. In my twenties, I began my career as an architect in the real estate market and working for Tishman Speyer, a prestigious international firm that manages properties around the globe, including Rockefeller Center. By the time I was thirty-five, I held a commercial senior management position; I also had a beautiful three-year-old daughter, Cora, and was pregnant with my second child.

I was very career-driven and during my first pregnancy I had worked up to the last week. Even during the maternity leave, I came into the office to continue some negotiations I was involved with. My second pregnancy, however, was different. I came down with pneumonia in the eighth month, and though my mind was still focused on work my body was telling me very clearly to stop. After giving birth, this time to a son, Josh, I took the full four months of maternity leave and dedicated myself completely to being a mom.

When I returned to the office, I was surprised to find the environment was quite different from the one I had left. My senior position was replaced by operational tasks and the space of connection that I used to have with the leadership was no longer available.

Data from a prominent university in Sao Paulo informs us that 48% of women are out of work within twenty-four months after coming back from maternity leave. And I became a statistic by leaving the senior position when I negotiated my resignation to leave the company.

After a few months of spending more time in traffic than with my kids and begging the nanny to keep my baby awake so I could get a goodnight kiss, I had realized I was not happy. I didn't know exactly what had changed inside me, but this hectic routine no longer made sense to me.

In January of 2017, I turned my energy to becoming an entrepreneur, and quickly realized that being a woman in the very male-dominated Brazilian real estate market was going to be a constant uphill battle. Within six months, I found myself trying to figure out something different to do with my experience and abilities.

A career transition—especially to a field outside the one you grew up in—is not a simple path. It's a marathon, and for me it would mean following my intuition, listening to my inner-knowing, and following the clues provided to me. I remember reading that the distance of a marathon, which had been forty kilometers since the first Olympic Games, was changed to twenty-six miles when they were held in London in 1908. What caught my interest, though, was that during those same games the distance was increased by another three hundred eighty-five yards. Why? The starting line was pulled back so children of Queen Alexandra could view it from the Royal Nursery at Windsor and Her Majesty could watch the finish at the White City Stadium in west London.

This sparked a curious connection in my mind. If that marathon could be altered so a mother (and queen) and her children could see the marathon, maybe I could find a way to include motherhood and my passion for work in the marathon of my life.

I began to immerse myself in female leadership studies and movements. I also became a member of Brazil's most prominent women's leadership group. One hundred thousand women strong, it is led by Luiza Helena Trajano, who was named by the *Financial Times* as one of the twenty-five most influential women in the world in 2021.

In that group I was able to feel more deeply into the lesson my fellow runner had taught me back in 2021: we are stronger when we run, and dream, together.

Also, it was during the meetings, and by communicating with other influencers, entrepreneurs, businesses, and empowering women, that I felt the need to create something dedicated to a specific sector, specifically, the real estate industry.

That feeling was connected to the numerous memories I had of being the only woman during my corporate experience. The only woman in the meeting room, the only woman at the construction field, the only woman during negotiations.

As my vision began to take shape, I was open to and invited

into my experience opportunities to integrate the feminine and the masculine, specifically in a business environment.

Now that I, "the student," was ready, "the masters" began to appear. It started with a message, sent by my then-husband, about an immersion seminar on Shakti leadership. He was the Director of Communications at the Brazilian Conscious Capitalism Chapter, and the organization was hosting a three-day experience with Nilima Bhat and Raj Sisodia, author of the book *Shakti Leadership: The Balance Between Male and Female Energy.*

That course was so intense for me. I remember crying most of the time, connecting both to my inner child and to the essence of the female energy more deeply. It was also during the Shakti immersion in Sao Paulo that I visualized myself doing the certification program on that leadership model, which was to begin in a month's time in San Diego. The knowing that I should do this was so strong that despite not having the money or time to travel, I was determined to find a way. It would be the first step in learning how to "walk the talk" of female leadership.

Financial challenges were nothing new to me. In fact, my difficult relationship with money had worked as an obstacle to reaching my goals and dreams. When I called Nilima to discuss the issues that were making my decision to go for the certification program harder, she told me that "money was the easiest part to solve." In accepting that challenge, I would have to do something I'd never done before: ask for help.

I called my uncle and asked to borrow the money, promising that I would pay him back within six months. He agreed, and one month after the immersion I was on a plane to San Diego. The training was amazing, and it was also where I found my soul sister, Rebecca Saltman.

After the conclusion of the certification program in Šibenik, Croatia, Nilima asked me whether I was planning to continue in the real estate industry, and how I would approach it.

British author and inspirational speaker Simon Sinek has said that leadership is to see a possible future and construct the path to be there. Nilima's unexpected question sparked the realization that I had lost the "key" I'd had to connect with this market and it was now necessary to create my own "door."

I began to see how the real estate industry would be more diverse, equal, and kind with women in it, and, one month after returning from Croatia I decided to found Mulheres do Imobiliário, "Women of Real Estate," which is Brazil's first female movement in the industry focused on empowering others.

In a little over two years, the movement has almost seven hundred members who are directly involved in providing sisterhood, mentoring, and focused training to women in the industry. It also offers scholarships for women whose careers were impacted by the pandemic to assist them in becoming real estate brokers. Like most countries around the world, Brazil's economy was hit hard by the pandemic, and this program opened doors for a new career that was lucrative and could be done from home. To date, the movement has provided scholarships to fifty women.

As my fortieth birthday approached my thoughts returned to my goal of running the New York City marathon. Though that hadn't happened, I had recently started running again, and was blessed with the opportunity to give my energy to an unknown woman struggling to reach the finish line, just as that woman had given her energy to me ten years earlier. Once again, I was amazed at how empowering it was to be able to cross that line together.

I was considering training for the New York City marathon again, and tackling some other things on my bucket list, such as climbing Mt. Everest, making the pilgrimage on the Camino Santiago, and returning to Machu Picchu. Then covid-19 happened, the world ground to a halt, and I found myself facing an internal crisis so deep that I asked my gynecologist if I was starting menopause—not surprising for someone so disconnected from her own body. I was not feeling any sexual desire and the energy that used to keep me enveloped in so many different projects now wasn't strong enough for even basic activities—being a present mother, for example.

In 2021, I began my first and most challenging marathon: the internal one. I spent a great deal of time reviewing my values, the purpose of my work, how I wanted to help women in the real estate industry moving forward, and even how I believed my kids should be educated in this changing world.

I was flooded with so many ideas that I decided to compile a book dedicated to the women who built their own patrimony (a word that ironically came from Old French *patrimoine*, from Latin *patrimonium*, from pater, *patr–* "father.") But I wasn't interested in talking about their property, a piece of land or a space in a building, but their internal landscape, one in which, as women, they build their own energetic foundations, pillars, and structures.

During the course of this project I learned that writing a book is a deep, transformative process, similar to birthing a child; it really changes us internally. I realized that we are all running life's marathons, and the only "winners" are those who look back and empower others to cross the finish lines.

Walking (or running) together is an act of empathy. It requires self-knowledge, self-empowerment, and the ability to truly see others, knowing that we are all connected.

By "seeing," what I really mean is connecting the dots. Remember those books or posters with different images that you fix your eyes to in order to "see" the other images contained within. That is my superpower—seeing through the images, situations, and information to find the truth inside. I know when to view things up close and when to step back to gain a different perspective. I understand when to look around me and give of myself to empower others.

As I look back on this journey, I am reminded of the article I read about lengthening the marathon to include the queen and her children. For me, it symbolizes opening the field for women and their families, and assisting them in charting a path in which they can nurture both their families and their own dream. This is my mission.

ABOUT THE AUTHOR: Elisa Tawil is a writer, mentor, and business consultant, and co-founder and leader of the Mulheres do Imobiliário, a movement committed to gender equity in the real estate industry. She has been named as one of LinkedIn's Top Voices and is a member of the Tiara Resource Circle. Elisa also serves as Counsellor of the NGO Gaia + and an executive at eXp Brasil. She is a columnist for *HSM Management Magazine, Imobi Report,* and *Exame Invest*, and the producer and presenter of the *Vieses Femininos* podcast. Elisa is the first certified Shakti Leader in São Paulo.

Elisa Tawil
elisatawil.com.br
mulheresdoimobiliario.com.br
elisa@elisatawil.com.br
+ 55 11 98884 7693

Turn Baby Turn

This practice is an easy way to boost the amount of energy in your body. It will also accelerate your positive emotions.

- Stand up and spread your arms out wide, making sure you have plenty of room to move in a full circle.

- To increase your energy, turn in a *clockwise* circle (to your right).* You can make it really simple by putting an object in your right hand and following it around.

- Your energy will amplify quickly. Go as fast or slow as feels good. You are no longer four years old, yet you can feel like it!

- Turn two times, then check in to see how you feel.

- Want more energy and a higher vibration? Spin a couple more times.

- Remember to check in with how you feel. A little Turn Baby Turn goes a long way!

Reverse it to Mellow in Moments

This is an effective way to decrease your energy, wind down, and be able to sit calmly in meetings or at other events.

- Turn in a *counterclockwise* circle (to your left).

- Notice as your body releases excess stored energy, allowing you to feel expansive.

- As in the original exercise, you can hold an object in your hand and follow it. This is also a magical way to calm down toddlers. Put a toy in their left hand and have them follow it around and bounce it off the bed until they feel like laying down to sleep.

- Enrich this practice by taking it outside to enjoy the grass under your feet, the wind in your hair, and the warmth of the sun on your face.

*If you are in a situation where you are unable to spin around with your whole body, you can move your hand in either the increase (right) or release (left) energy direction and still experience the results. This also works great when you are in a meeting. You can do it by moving your hands under the table, or even by twiddling your thumbs!

** If it feels like the directions are reversed for you, that's fine. Just trust which way you turn to increase or decrease the energy in your body and energy field.

CHAPTER 17

Tuning My Antennae
Dana Micheli

"**D**ana is a very difficult child to parent. Her antennae are always up, so she hears things you are not even saying."

These words, spoken by my psychiatrist during a family therapy session, was the first time anyone had described me as an "empath," though it would be decades before I heard that term or understood the impact it has had on my life. Still, my seventeen-year-old self, hospitalized for four months for an eating disorder, knew she was not saying this in a derogatory way, but simply trying to give my frantic parents some small measure of peace. I was not surprised that she said I was difficult, only surprised and intrigued by how much the antennae part resonated.

It seemed that ever since I was a small child, I had been able to sense what those close to me were feeling—particularly when those feelings were of sadness or loneliness—and do everything in my power to fix it. This often—especially with my peers—showed up as me downplaying any abilities or advantages I had and playing up their own.

I also from a young age had a need for a great deal of time alone. My family, both nuclear and extended, was close; I had friends too, and enjoyed spending time with them all. Still, I always looked forward to those moments when I walked into the woods behind our yard or read a book in my room late at night until my eyes crossed from exhaustion. Those walks were my version of a religious experience, those books were my escape into worlds more exciting and real than my own. As a kid, I thought this meant I was a weirdo, a loner—I mean, who doesn't want to be surrounded by people all the time? While reasonable minds may still disagree as to my level of "weirdness," at the time I didn't realize that I just needed that alone time to recharge.

How I ended up starving myself, well, there were a few reasons for that, and none of them had anything to do with looking like a supermodel. In actuality, I didn't care how I looked to other people, only how I felt, which was in control of my environment (body)… until the disease took control of me. What I learned from that very talented and caring psychiatrist (who I would learn many years later is an empath and medium herself), is that the anorexia was a way of numbing all the feelings – my own and those I picked up from others. It's hard to care about much else when your mind is constantly engaged in figuring out the calories of everything that passes your lips—even a tomato slice or stick of gum was accounted for—or not even taking a second to breathe before jumping on the stationary bike after school.

She also cautioned me against becoming a "dry drunk"—which she termed as being a recovering alcoholic who abstains from drink but engages in the behaviors surrounding it, such as codependency. I knew intellectually what she was talking about, but frankly, at the time my only worry was how I could gain just enough weight to get out of the hospital and still be able to see my bones. Indeed, most of my time there was spent trying to circumvent the protocols; I would do as I had always done—be perfectly compliant to everyone's faces, then secretly exercise in my room at night and hide my Ensures in my closet. Yet, I was eventually released, and by the grace of God (and unlike many of my fellow patients), never had to be readmitted. Life continued—college, law school, relationships (some toxic, some wonderful), and I thought, *I am cured.*

During those years I noticed I had the ability to sense when a guy

I dated was lying, or a stranger—despite their chipper smile—was a "hot mess" and not to be trusted. Yet though I liked and found this interesting, I didn't connect to those "antennae" my doctor had mentioned. It was also something I had to defend when people in my family thought I was "jumping to conclusions" or "being judgmental." These assessments always turned out to be true, though sometimes it took quite a while to be revealed. I remember telling my mother I didn't like a new friend she had made—there was something not stable inside, something not quite right. She felt like a drain. My mother insisted she was a lovely woman—just "going through a lot"—right up to the moment, fifteen years later, when her friend did her wrong.

I often ignored these knowings when it came to the people I encountered, and it was many years before I realized I was indeed the dry drunk—eating each day but alternatively pleasing and withdrawing from others. I was definitely not managing their energy or mine in a healthy manner. I also downplayed my own value both personally and professionally, feared that I would be suffocated by any real romantic commitment, and generally edited my dreams to fit what I believed to be possible, given my "weirdness." And that's when the real work, and an incredible journey, began.

I didn't set out to be a writer, though I had always loved writing and was encouraged to do so by my teachers. To me it was one of those pipedreams that, except for a small few (certainly not me!), would lead nowhere. Law was much safer and had always been an interest as well; moreover, my decision to attend law school satisfied the Type A person in me, as well as the one who needed to feel normal and on purpose. The reality turned out to be far different, and long before graduation I was announcing that I no longer wanted to be an attorney. On this I was very clear—it wasn't that I didn't enjoy the material or thinking critically, but because I couldn't stomach the "environment" (aka energy). A short stint at a firm later confirmed my observations at school, and within a year I was having all kinds of physical symptoms, including heaviness in my chest, that magically disappeared the day I walked out of there for good.

Flash forward several years and several crappy jobs later, I met a woman via Facebook who was hiring an editor for her writing business. As it turned out, the vast majority of her clients were mediums, walk-ins, energy healers, and empaths, all of whom would unknowingly become my teachers. Through these incredible people, I learned about doing the real inner work (i.e., through meditation) needed to cure my "dry drunkenness." So much of the way I had handled my life, primarily my relationships, now made sense. (Interestingly, the woman who hired me, who's also an intuitive and a healer, was the first person to call me an empath. I immediately googled the word as soon as I read her email!).

Something else also became apparent over the years of doing this work—my sensitivity allows me to step into the "feels" of my clients. Whether I was ghostwriting a book from scratch or editing a manuscript, I started hearing, "How do you do that? It was like I wrote the words myself!"—and I started to realize that I was "reading" them, through our phone conversations and even emails. Just recently I had to laugh (to myself) when a client referred to my "second sight" with regard to our work together. Just as importantly, this led me to a soul tribe I never would have otherwise met, one that includes Sue Urda and Kathy Fyler of Powerful You! Publishing, and their many authors, with whom I have been blessed to work with for many years.

Managing my sensibility is still very much a work in progress. For example, it is only over the past few years that I realize how deeply I am affected by what I read, hear, and see. I now shy away from sad novels, whereas I used to devour them; TV shows that have too much violence or are about true crimes I avoid, knowing watching them is the equivalent of wearing a dark heavy cloak for days. Far more challenging is learning how to process "real-life" things in a healthy way, and when something, be it good or challenging, happens I remind myself to look at how I really feel, rather than trying to numb it or allowing it to overwhelm me.

Most importantly, this journey has made me aware of my enormous capacity for joy—it is my setpoint and greater than any discomfort or pain I feel. I also have the ability to shift my energy by doing the simplest of things—taking a walk along the tree-lined streets of my Brooklyn neighborhood or bathing in the delicious buzz of Manhattan, laughing with friends or my mom, or listening to my cat purr. I can also see with clarity the many blessings in my life, including being able to use my ability as an empath to do the work I love so much.

ABOUT THE AUTHOR: Dana Micheli is a ghostwriter, editor, and owner of Writers in the Sky Creative Writing Services. She has ghostwritten and edited nonfiction and fiction books across several genres, including memoirs and multigenerational family sagas; business and legal matters; science fiction/fantasy; romance and crime; however, most of her projects fall along the spiritual spectrum. Before pursuing her writing career full-time, Dana served as a lobbyist on behalf of the Arizona Coalition Against Domestic Violence and as the Manager of PR/Communications for The New York Women's Foundation. Dana has a B.A. in English from Southern Connecticut University and a Juris Doctor from New York Law School. She lives in Brooklyn, New York.

Dana Micheli
Writers in the Sky
writersinthesky.com

EMPATH TOOL
by Jade Rehder

Filter It Out!

This practice is used to create an agreement with your energy bodies and entire field so you stay out of the effects of toxic environments and overlays of energy that come through the collective, electronic transmissions (online, radio, et cetera), other people, and so much more!

- Imagine a thick filter made of the elements of creation (fire, water, wind, earth, and spirit); the metals of the Earth (gold, silver, copper, lead, titanium, platinum, et cetera); and anything else you are guided to add. Think of this like a multidimensional HEPA filter that keeps out all energy pollutants.

- Ask the filter to wrap around your energy field and form three-hundred and sixty degrees of protection around you.

- Now, ask the filter to lock in place and remain active in your field, round the clock, every day, while you are awake and asleep.

- Ask the filter to self-clean.

- Remember, you are still receiving the energy that supports and assists you to create synergy, grow, and evolve.

CHAPTER 18

My Many Flavors of Knowing
Jade Rehder

It's been a lifelong negotiation between my spiritual gifts—those of knowing, feeling, sensing, and seeing things before they happen (not to mention the full-on team of voices in my head)—and my human personality. It usually boils down to what I am willing to do or not do, and there have been many times when I said no or ignored my guidance altogether.

I was five when I had a vision that we would lose our new black, curly-haired puppy if my brother got to hold it. I attempted to tell my mom yet at the time lacked the tools to explain what I was so clearly seeing in my head. The experience of the visceral and painful gut response to knowing what would happen, and watching it play out, had a huge impact on me and my willingness to share what I knew. I either kept quiet or engaged in over-explaining, which can exhaust others and is just one way I gave away my power.

During my elementary school years I had a few memorable experiences, like knowing a groom was abusive to the bride and they shouldn't get married, or that certain adults were cheating on their spouses. When I shared this information I was told I didn't know what I was talking about. The truth always came out, yet these and the many other times I was misunderstood led me, at ten years old, to shut off my inner vision and telepathy. I even remember the month and year this happened: November 1976. It was a cold, snowy day in northern Minnesota, and we were inside for recess. I recall slamming down a doll and saying to myself that I was too old for child's play. I then imagined myself turning a knob to click off the outer voices. Then I saw a light switch and I imagined turning it off. Yes, I was very thorough, and shut down my natural abilities completely—well, almost completely. I still had my ultra-sensitive feeling capacity and the ever-present team of voices channeling in without being so overwhelmed all the time. Shortly thereafter, my moon arrived, signaling the start of my maiden's journey. As many of us know, our natural intuitive psychic gifts increase when we transition from child to maiden. I would wait until I was thirty-three years old to turn those gifts back on.

Fast forward to June 21, 2001. I'm in a car with my former husband, my brother, and his new girlfriend, and we're headed for Canyon City, Colorado to go whitewater river rafting. This is my first meeting with the girlfriend, and I'm excited to find that she's a great listener, because I totally want to tell her all his embarrassing stories! I'm talking non-stop when I suddenly hear the voice in my head that sounds like Charlton Heston when he was in the role of Moses. This voice is somewhat familiar—for me it's like the Holy Spirit—and now it's saying that we will be in a wreck on our way back in Castle Rock. When I ignore the voice—after all, I'm in the middle of a story—a picture of a construction sign bearing the same message in hot pink letters flashes in my mind. I ignore it again, and it repeats in bright blue letters. After getting the message three times within thirty seconds, I literally throw my right hand up into the air and say inside my head, "Can't you see I'm busy down here telling a story!" (Ironic, since much of my work today is walking people out of their old stories.)

Until I started working with clients in 1999, I'd thought everyone had a team of voices in their head. Then people started asking me who the heck were the "They" that I spoke of often during my sessions. THEY is the team of my continuum of consciousness, or what you might call high selves, angels, guides, or ancestors. I'm a conscious channel.

Astrology has also played an ancillary role in my awareness of self. Five of my planets, including my sun, are in Pisces, which contributes to the natural flow of intuitive information and allows me to be very comfortable with the dream world and concepts that can be difficult to understand. Plus I have an Aries moon, which governs the highly sensitive emotional body that has led me most of my life. It's also why I have spent twenty-plus years working primarily with the emotion-set. My ascendant sign (how you show up in the outer world) is high-degree Scorpio, which has me desiring to transcend and alchemize low vibrations as quickly as the phoenix.

Back to that fateful car ride and the repeated messages from "Charlton Heston." I chose to disregard, never mentioning what I had heard to anyone else. In fact, exhausted from our rafting excursion, I had dozed off before we drove through Castle Rock on our way home. The damage to our bodies from the accident was far less severe than what you would guess by the look of my brother's totaled Jeep. I'm here today because the voice in my head literally woke me up right before the vehicle rear-ended us, crashing into the exact spot where my head was resting. I had chosen to ignore it, then I chose to listen, and it saved my life.

That experience, now more than two decades ago, was a huge turning point, and what I learned from it still benefits me today. I was forced to slow down. I had to let go of control and give other people massive authority in my construction business, of which I had previously been a complete micromanager. I learned I am no fan of pharmaceuticals. I saw kindness from people I had no idea cared about me. Most importantly, I learned that when my guidance is asking me to listen and gives me a message three times, there's going to be a huge learning if I choose to ignore it. I have called this my "cosmic two-by-four with railroad spikes."

Honestly, I still miss the mark sometimes with what my guidance tells me, though I am listening to it more and more.

That event also brought me back to the path I had walked as a child. There have been countless awarenesses along the way; for example, I was unaware until 2005 that there was a name for someone who picks up energies the way I do, let alone that the name was "empath." Having a word to describe the way I receive energy helped me to start working consciously to create practices and daily routines that allow me and my clients to navigate our Earth experience with more ease. To date, I have scripted over eighty personal energy practices (many included in this book) from numerous sources, including my high selves.

In 2016 I received a call from a friend who told me he knew how to clear our ego conditioning. He instructed me to use some energy forms we had been experimenting with from the seventh dimension of consciousness and beyond. I was to think about it for four days, then do it if I got a "yes." Well, I had no need to wait—I had an immediate body response and my knowing gave me a yes right away. Twenty minutes later I did the practice and knocked myself out cold! When I woke up I heard, *This is a gift you will take out into the world!* From this experience the KLEAR Channel modality was born. It has evolved and improved over the years, and is one of the most effective tools to transcend stored energies and mental, emotional, and physical conditioning that I and many of my clients have experienced. It creates a space of freedom to receive the clear message behind the conditioning, allowing you to learn, remember, or become aware of it so you are in your power of choice. And, as the KLEAR transmission flows through my voice and presence virtually as well as in person, it has indeed allowed me to help more people than ever before through online work.

The last time I missed the "big message" was the summer of 2020. One night I was startled awake by a voice that screamed in my head, "FIRE!" and I sat straight up in bed like I had the abs of a fifteen-year-old. The need to look outside was really strong, so I walked to the front of my house and opened the door. The smell of smoke was no surprise; after all, it was wildfire season and in the Rouge Valley we'd had smoke in the air for over three months already. I did a one-eighty scan for a red glow and distinctly remember my eyes resting for a beat in this one area to my far left. Seeing no active fire, I headed back into the house and heard, clear as day, "Get prepared, Jade." My immediate thought was, *I will after my one p.m. client tomorrow,* then I went back to bed and fell asleep. The next morning, while having tea with a shaman friend, I got a phone call from my mom, who told me a fire was spreading just north of Ashland, which was where my home was. Later, I would find out that the fire started in the exact spot I had been looking at the night before. I was safe and so were all the people in my neighborhood; our homes, however, were a different story. At one o'clock, instead of meeting with a client, I was standing on top of a hill watching black smoke emanate from the area where my house used to be.

The lesson, while difficult, was very clear. I missed a really important part of that message by thinking I knew when to prepare, and following my own will rather than the loving voice guiding me. If I had only asked the question, "Do I act now, or do I have some time?", I could have saved some beautiful things. Instead, I was left with what was in my car, plus the powerful realization that my value is greater than my material things. Value is an inside job! This experience also reminded me that tuning into my inner knowing and feeling is what allowed me to have a response system with my high self. I had overridden my system by deciding that I "had time."

This journey has been greater than the challenges, of course, and also filled with fun and joyous creations that came from following my knowing. On Thanksgiving Day 2021, I was driving through downtown Florence, a tourist spot on the Central Oregon coast, where I live now (one of the positive outcomes from the fire in 2020). Suddenly I had this spontaneous thought, accompanied by a flood of yummy feelings in my body. What would it be like if someone leased a store on Bay Street, filled it with rocks, and let me come and be one of the main people who shares the magic of crystals and stones with the world? I voiced this "creation request" with my Sweetheart, all the while watching the ripples of energy flow.

When I got home, I heard, "Get on Facebook." My human mind said no, as I'd already had my "Facebook time" that day. Then I heard it again—"Go to Facebook!"—and reluctantly did as I was told. Next I heard, "Go to your Florence group." There, I saw a post from earlier that morning: "Looking for someone with retail experience and knowledge of crystals..." Ding, ding, ding—that's me!

I directly messaged the man and, come to find out, he's a friend of a friend of mine. She had actually attempted to connect us in June and at the time it didn't flow. Now it certainly was flowing, and on the Sunday after Thanksgiving I drove down to meet him at his rock shop in Bandon. There's a story behind even getting me out the door for that meeting because he has an Aries sun sign like my first husband and I had a lot of junk running about doing anything with another Aries male. This time I tapped into my knowing, got over all of that stuff, and got on with it. Knowing that people can be different than we expect and project onto them is one of the biggest awarenesses and most wonderful opportunities we have in this life. You may be reading this book while I'm standing in Crystal Aloha—manifested because I listened to my knowing!

I leave you with words I wish I had heard earlier on my path. As you expand and grow, you will acquire views that may make it appear to your "knower self" that your past self and choices were "wrong." I encourage you to see the journey as a hike through a vast wilderness, where you will oftentimes be unable to see the trail ahead. Ask yourself the question, "Can I give myself permission to leave the missteps in the past?" Know that I have, and you can too! Embrace the moment and allow yourself to know from your integrated self (through your heart) that life is a journey, with more flavors of experience ahead.

ABOUT THE AUTHOR: Jade's heart longing is that the world accesses the absolute love available within ~ Aloha. As an energy alchemist (healer) and self-actualization guide, Jade has led more than eight hundred trainings and retreats since 1999. She creates the space for you to walk out of the chaos and confusion, clean up your emotion-set, and build your trust muscle so you can take your Spirit-led work out in the world. She assists others in accessing their inner magic through her innate intuitive gifts enhanced with advanced training in Hawaiian Huna la'au kahea, multiple energy modalities, neurolinguistics, voice alchemy, breathwork, and sound. Dancing ~ Joying ~ Being.

Jade Rehder
Do You Feel Different
Jade@JadeRehder.com
JadeRehder.com
YouTube: JadeRehderLightMessengerAlchemist

EMPATH TOOL
by Jade Rehder

Turn It Over

Have you ever said or thought to yourself, "Part of me wants to do this and part of me wants to do this other thing?" Have you experienced conflict in a personal or work relationship that appears unresolvable? In my experience, using this practice is like a magic potion to release that conflict and create harmony.

Turn It Over integrates energetic or emotional parts within you or with others with whom you are experiencing a conflict, challenges, or feeling in opposition to. The goal is to surrender the work to God/Creator/The Divine/The Universe to do the work at a quantum level, allowing you to relax and notice the changes.

- Sit down and close your eyes.

- Put your hands palm up on your knees.

- Ask which hand the conflicting energy wants to be in and intend/see/feel/pretend the conflict energy is in that hand.

- Put the energy of your desire/want/resolution/solution in the other hand.

- Now ask/command the energy to flow up your arm and see/feel/imagine/pretend it is doing so, coming together in your heart space as you take a deep breath in.

- Notice how your hands want to come together over your heart. Bring them there and exhale.

- Breathe in and move the energy up into your throat area and exhale.

- Now breathe in and send the energy out the top of your head to your high self.

- Exhale and allow the energy to go all the way to God/Creator/The Divine/The Universe.

- Turn over the work to be done at a quantum level, beyond space and time.

- Notice how all energy is one at this level of consciousness.

- Now come back fully into your body and this moment.

You have Turned It Over! Well done!

CHAPTER 19

Know Thyself
Catherine Ann Wright

If you are reading this book, you are what I call an "Experiencer"—you are seeking answers as to why you see the world so differently. And, no matter how this book found its way into your hands, it is by no coincidence or accident. You have manifested it and ME—"U Empath You."

On this Earth-school journey, I have been extremely protected by some powerful, supernatural, loving forces, yet I have felt extremely alone in discovering and experiencing my abilities. Certainly, the fear of judgment for being different silenced me. But like Neo in the movie, *The Matrix*, I learned the key to thriving on this plane is to "Temet Nosce" ("Know Thyself") and normalize paranormal stories.

Precognitive/Clairaudient

An experience at the age of sixteen, upgraded my belief systems and changed my life. I was driving to school when I heard a voice very calmly and plainly say, "Slow down, a dog is coming out from between the cars." I reiterated the thought back to myself as a clear possibility: "I had better slow down because a dog might come out from between the cars." Sure enough, as I began to gently brake, a real-live dog came out from between two parked cars! It was unbelievable how close I came to having a terrible accident. This precognitive incident made such an impression on me. I started to really listen to this Voice that was clearly different than my own self-speak. It was as if a loving grandparent or teacher was training me to listen. I realized that over the course of my life, it had been giving me lesson after lesson so I could learn to trust this inner, knowing-self.

Clear Touch/ Psychometry/Clairaudient

In 2004, I purchased a house that unbeknownst to me was very haunted. I remember stepping out of the realtor's car, and—as my foot touched the ground—I heard a voice say, clear as day, "This is your home." I felt a rush of excitement hearing this familiar voice I trusted. I went around the house adventurously looking in every cabinet and turning on every water nozzle, knowing this was going to be my new home. After I left that property, another realtor called to show me three other homes, and I went with him thinking it was logical to know all my options. As we viewed the other homes, I suddenly got shoulder pain so severe I had to leave. I called my massage therapist, who said firmly, "Why are you looking at other homes? Weren't you told you found it already?!"

Clearly, I was getting another sign that the first home was for me. I had no idea that the shoulder pain was an experience of physical mediumship; or that I was about to step into an advanced, fourteen-year, metaphysical course in inner-dimensional, psychic and spiritual training. After countless paranormal experiences, I did research. I learned that more than forty people had brutally died close to my boundary line and hundreds more died on the surrounding area. My property resided on intersecting major and minor ley-lines on an active underground lakebed creating portals. Kinetically, this allowed the dead (disincarnates) and interdimensional beings of lower vibrations to travel to and traverse my home from one-hundred-fifty miles away as if on a freeway. Sounds like a scary movie, right? I was so far behind in my evolution that my higher-self and spirit guides decided to slap me awake with a psychic smack-down haunted house experience.

Chapter 19
Know Thyself

Clairaudience

One time, while in the master bedroom, I heard chatter—like a group of people talking about me. I heard the spirits laugh and say, "She is Morgan La Fae." I yelled out "STOP LAUGHING AT ME!" Then, I listened to the inner voice telling me to research that name. Imagine my shock when the Google search of "Morgan La Fae" led to this past-life or simultaneous-life avatar of mine (In quantum theory, linear time is an illusion, and theoretically all timelines are happening simultaneously.) I began laughing with the disincarnates, for they were not scary at all but helping me learn. "Karmically" or subconsciously, I married a man whose name led me to my simultaneous, sorcerous avatar abilities. Just as important, I realized that getting TRIGGERED plus RESEARCH equaled CLEARED EMOTIONS in the now. I became interested in uncovering other simultaneous avatars which led me to my regression, Quantum Hypnosis journey; henceforth, I am seeing the immediate release (canceling-out) of dis-EASES and traumas.

Projective Empath

Have you ever heard the saying, "We create our own realities?" Having the "projective empath" skillset, I literally create realities by projecting emotional energy onto others and the world. LESSON: By emotionally feeling so different, I merged being brutally bullied in other past lives to this present life. This resulted in my being bullied by society, by the corporate world, by my family, and by my peers. I tracked down this life's original rejection "program," which started right from birth with parental rejection. I was a highly sensitive baby, so imagine the energetic trauma as my crazy mother reiterated my birth story. She told me she had freaked out that I was a redhead and not a brunette like the rest of the family. She even yelled at the hospital staff, "This is not my baby!" and ordered them to foot-print me again. Talk about a fairy changeling syndrome!

Later, when I tried to share my empathic secrets, my mother's exact judgmental, Christian words were: "I can't talk to you if you talk to dead people!" My response: "Read your bible, MOTHER! Jesus spoke to the dead and cast out demons, also!" In the meantime, she was also slandering me to the family, saying I was mentally ill even though my doctors confirmed otherwise (I later realized she was projecting, for I am a Heyoka empath, or a spiritual mirror to those around me.) When she died in 2021, she left every child a personal letter. Mine said that I may benefit from psychiatric medication—a final act of projection on her part.

I was strongly programmed by family and religion to believe that if you hear voices, you are mentally ill; and that, paranormal phenomena are hoaxes and just plain weird. Talking of such things would label me as an occultist which in turn triggered my rejection programs. I know now that empaths are brilliant at tapping into multi-consciousness frequencies.

These rejection programs and artificial belief systems kept me in a lower emotional vibration for much of my life. From these abusive programs, I learned to transcend, transmute, and reformat the emotional root triggers like computer software on a hard drive. Whether these emotions/programs are mine or someone else's, they still have to be processed and cleared. As a regression hypnotist, I have learned that if unprocessed, emotions get stuck in my body and cellular memory complex and they can cause extreme discomfort and dis-EASE; or, the emotional programs can be flipped and used for healing.

Physical Mediumship

The shoulder pain—I felt while viewing the homes in 2004— was just one example of physical manifestation of messages and energies. At the age of thirty-three, I was ruled disabled and had to leave an incredible government job due to fibromyalgia. Baffled by this mysterious disease, doctors at one point decided it was all in the patient's head. Eventually, however, there were so many people presenting with these symptoms that they could no longer dismiss them. Fibromyalgia taught me that negative emotions (mine or others') crippled me if I don't manage my energetic field. Empaths are hypersensitive to energy frequencies. Thus, I have learned that joyful, appreciative emotions regenerate, recalibrate, transmute, transcend, and clear the negative ones. And finally, I learned about boundaries. As an empath, I was an enabler without boundaries (energetic or otherwise). I always wanted to please and almost never said no, hence I attracted narcissists as lovers and friends. In order to survive, I learned to listen to that "inner-voice" and to practice trust, and release my control issues so I could receive and believe the messages without filters.

The Collective/Mass Consciousness

Later on in my journey, I learned that some of my thoughts and feelings may not be mine but those of mass consciousness: be it human or—far worse—demonic/malevolent entities who have found their way onto this plane. I had to become an expert on frequencies and spirits.

In November 2015, I suddenly began crying hysterically with no idea why. It continued for two days before I learned that there had been a series of coordinated terrorist attacks in Paris, France. Well, I am very connected to France—and Paris in particular—as I studied at the Sorbonne in 1991 and have had many past-lives there. I was actually feeling the horror of the French mass consciousness all the way to my home in Salem, Oregon. Once I heard about the attacks, I realized what was going on and could stop the emotion. When I know "why" something is making me feel or think a certain way, then I understand the game—the electromagnetic process of being connected to the "ALL THAT IS"; then, I can adjust the frequency, the belief, or the perception to clear the Mind/Body/ Spirit complex to a neutral mindset with toolbox techniques I have learned or created for myself.

Receptive/Emotional Empath

I must constantly monitor my thoughts, beliefs, and feelings to discern what is mine and what belongs to visitors, neighbors, lovers, and so on. I have felt suicidal thoughts and acute anger only to find out later that someone I was connected with was feeling that way. At times, these thoughts certainly felt like mine which confused and overwhelmed me because suicide and anger are not my emotional complexes.

One day at home, I suddenly felt this rush of psychotic anger. I looked out the window to see my then-husband and his co-worker arguing. The co-worker was clearly irate; I realized it was this person's emotions I was feeling. I went out and diffused the situation with a big hug and greeting and told them to take it to the office. They did, but I couldn't forget that feeling of overpowering rage. I didn't even know this kind of anger existed! Intuitively, I knew I had to work on releasing this emotion so as not to take it on as my own. To this day, when I feel dark emotions, I immediately feel into them; I figure out if they belong to me, and if necessary, take appropriate action. These remarkable self-discoveries and lessons have greatly facilitated my work as a healer and hypnotist helping people to clear their own belief systems and traumas.

Earth School Is Tough

It wasn't until 2013 that I even heard the terms: empath, sensitive, ESP, psychic medium, ETs, aliens, UFOs, ghosts, poltergeists, shamans, hauntings, or any of the "clairs" (clairvoyant, clairaudient and so on). I certainly didn't know I was a sensitive empath! Thankfully, Source led me to a TV series called, "The Dead Files." Amy Allan (a physical medium) and Steve DiSchiavi (a retired New

York City homicide detective) team up to investigate the paranormal, including haunted houses. Had it not been for this show, I would still be in a very uneducated, dark place unable to explain the thousands of experiences I have witnessed.

So, as I traverse new cycles of evolution occurring on this planet, I "Know Thyself" and I am not alone. This realization has opened my consciousness to a plethora of abilities and realities. Most importantly, I have learned to LOVE myself as a unique individual. And, as an "Experiencer," I know that if we normalize empathic experiences from childhood, others will not have to suffer in silent ignorance of these abilities. We are long overdue in freeing ourselves from judgment and in seeing these abilities as blessings and natural expressions of our authentic and sovereign selves. We are meant to survive and thrive in full expression without fear.

ABOUT THE AUTHOR: Catherine Ann Wright is a Quantum Regression Hypnotist (Delores Cannon and Alba Weinman methods), Harmonic Sound Healer, Source Alchemist, Grid Worker, Medium and Channel, Demonologist, Galactic Historian, teacher, author, and UFO researcher and experiencer. She studied at the University of Southern California in Los Angeles and the Sorbonne in Paris, and holds a Doctor of Divinity. Previously, she worked for state and federal government agencies, hospitals, doctors, attorneys, real estate developers, and Anheuser Busch in marketing. Catherine's passions are to secure health for her clients by sharing how to Unlearn, how to manipulate the matrices of Earthly operating systems, clearing old programs and written and oral storytelling.

Catherine Ann Wright
503-856-4855 (Call or text preferable)
CatherineAnnWright.com
CatsWildRide.com
YouTube: Search Catherine Ann Wright

Unplug Method

This is an excellent, self-guided process for allowing limiting beliefs and excess energies to leave the body. It is best to do on your own when you are in a good and stable state of mind and body. I also suggest recording the steps on your phone beforehand, including time for silence, to more easily guide yourself.

First, name and write down the limiting belief or negatively-charged past experience you are unplugging.

Choose your new belief or how you want to feel about the past experience and write it down.

Now ask, "Body/mind, do I have 100% agreement to let go of the excess energy connected to (insert what you're unplugging)?

When you receive permission from your inner guidance, you may begin the process.

Adjust the Visual Screen

- Close your eyes.

- Create a visual symbol (shape, movie, or collage of images) to represent this specific limiting belief or past experience. Put the symbol on an imaginary whiteboard at arm's length in front of you. Allow all the visual triggers and cues included in the energy to flow out to your whiteboard. On a conscious level, you may be unable to keep up with what your body/mind sends out, and that is alright. This will only take a minute or two.

- Stop all movement and take a color screenshot of what's on the whiteboard.
- Now, turn the screenshot black and white and make it dull and flat.

Delete Your Audio Track

- Hear what you are saying to yourself while running the limiting belief or recalling the experience.
- What are others saying that relates to or triggers this belief or memory?
- Send the sounds out onto the whiteboard.
- In your mind's eye, turn the volume control knob for these sounds to the OFF position. Hear it CLICK off.

Let Go of the Energy of the Feelings and Emotions

- What energy are you feeling in your body connected to this belief or experience?
- Send those that no longer serve you out onto the whiteboard.
- Breathe in deeply through your nose and exhale strongly out your mouth four times, allowing the energy of those feelings and emotions to leave from your body/mind. Do sets of four breaths until you feel the energy is gone.
- Now, turn the feeling control knob (for these energies) in your mind completely OFF. Hear and feel the CLICK.
- Go to the whiteboard and turn it all black. Imagine shrinking it down to the size of a period.
- Envision picking up this dot and tossing it over your shoulder so it bounces like a ball off the end of the Earth.
- Notice the energy shift? How do you feel?

About the Authors

**Are you inspired by the stories in this book?
Let the authors know.**

**See the contact information at the end of each chapter
and reach out to them.**

They'd love to hear from you!

Author Rights & Disclaimer

*Each author in this book retains the copyright and all inherent
rights to their individual chapter. Their stories are printed herein
with each author's permission.*

*Each author is responsible for the individual opinions expressed
through their words. Powerful You! Publishing bears no
responsibility for the content of the stories by these authors.*

Acknowledgements

ac·knowl·edg·ment
/əkˈnäləjmənt/
noun: acknowledgement: an author's or publisher's statement of indebtedness to others, typically one printed at the beginning of a book.

That statement, however, takes on a more prominent meaning when the compiling, editing, and publishing of a book was handled by empaths.

One thing we believe all empaths have in common is a sense of feeling "things" deeply, which Oxford describes as "the ability to apprehend the mental or emotional state of another individual." We are also "wired" to be profoundly aware of those who touch our lives, even in the smallest of ways, and be in a constant state of acknowledgement and appreciation of them. All this to say that if we were to individually thank everyone who helped us get this book to the finish line, it would be another full book in itself, AND we would very much like to express our deepest gratitude to the people without whom *U Empath You* would still be a project in our heads.

First, to ALL of the contributing authors! You and your stories are the magic that has created a much-needed wave of support for all who engage with this book. Your vulnerability in telling your life experiences will inspire others to also open up and share things often unspoken and know that they are no longer alone. You are truly way-showers and bringers of Light in this world!

To our beloved editor, Dana Micheli: You are a word alchemist!

Your empathic gifts, deep knowing, sense of humor, and overall delight has made this seemingly impossible task possible for us, and for that we are so deeply grateful.

To our trainers, AmondaRose Igoe, Kathy Sipple, Karen Flaherty, and Francine Sinclair—your knowledge, generosity, and wisdom created a beautiful container for our sensitive crew and you made the work so much more generative, thank you!

To Sue Urda and Kathy Fyler of Powerful You! Publishing—we wonder if we have enough room to describe all of our thanks for making this process accessible to two novices like us. We are eternally grateful for helping ALL of us get this out into the world.

We also must thank each other, because we could never have done it on our own!

Most of all, we would like to acknowledge the initiations, as they were a true gift and the flow of spirit and creativity that has been the unseen companion of this entire endeavor.

Deep thanks and Mahalo Nui Loa
Jade and Rebecca

You Matter by BEing You.
Breathe it in.

What the world needs is LOVE
And Empaths have the power.

About
Rebecca Saltman and Jade Rehder

We have known one another for many lifetimes, in this incarnation and others! From nonprofit organizations to roofing companies and Disrupting for Good to Energy Alchemy, we have been through it together.

To learn about anything created by the ripple effect of this book and our other latest shenanigans, please see here:

Rebecca

https://disruptforgood.life

Jade

https://jaderehder.com

Check out what's happening
https://uempathyou.com

Powerful You! Publishing
Sharing Wisdom ~ Shining Light

Are You Called to be an Author?

If you're like most people, you may find the prospect of writing a book daunting. Where to begin? How to proceed? No worries! We're here to help.

Whether you choose to contribute to an anthology or write your own book, we're here for you. We'll be your guiding light, professional consultant, and enthusiastic supporter. If you see yourself as an author partnering with a publishing company who has your best interest at heart and expertise to back it up, we'd be honored to be your publisher.

We provide personalized guidance through the writing and editing process, as well as many necessary tools for your success as an author. We offer complete publishing packages and our service is designed for a personal and optimal author experience.

We are committed to helping individuals express their voice and shine their light into the world. Are you ready to start your journey as an author? Do it with Powerful You! Publishing.

Powerful You! Publishing
239-280-0111
powerfulyoupublishing.com